TO LIVE AND DIE
IN THE WEST

THE AMERICAN INDIAN WARS

TO LIVE AND DIE IN THE WEST

THE AMERICAN INDIAN WARS

JASON HOOK · MARTIN PEGLER

COLOUR ILLUSTRATIONS BY
CHRISTA HOOK, PETER SARSON,
DAVID SQUE & RICHARD HOOK

First published in 1999 by Osprey Publishing,
Elms Court, Chapel Way, Botley, Oxford OX2 9LP
Email: osprey@osprey-publishing.co.uk

Previously published as Warrior 4 *US Cavalryman 1865–1890*,
Men-at-Arms 163 *The American Plains Indians* and
Men-at-Arms 186 *The Apaches*

ISBN 1 84176 018 8

Editors: Marcus Cowper and Nikolai Bogdanovic
Filmset in Singapore by Pica Ltd
Cover and new pages filmset by Imaging and Art Studios
Printed in China through World Print Ltd

99 00 01 02 03   10 9 8 7 6 5 4 3 2 1

FOR A CATALOGUE OFF ALL TITLES PUBLISHED BY
OSPREY MILITARY, AUTOMOTIVE AND AVIATION PLEASE WRITE TO:

Osprey Direct UK, PO Box 140, Wellingborough,
Northants NN8 4ZA, UK
Email: info@OspreyDirect.co.uk

Osprey Direct USA, P.O. Box 130, Sterling Heights,
MI 48311-0130, USA
Email: info@OspreyDirectUSA.com

Or visit the Osprey website at: *http://www.osprey-publishing.co.uk*

Page 2
**A staged studio portrait of Shun-ka Blo-ka or 'He-Dog' of the
Oglala Sioux. (Smithsonian Institution)**

CONTENTS

US CAVALRYMAN

INTRODUCTION

This section is not a history of the Indian Wars, nor of the Army as a whole. Rather, it is an attempt to convey to the reader the reality of campaign service of just one part of the United States Army – that of the US Cavalry.

Over the years, the US Cavalry has been glamorised and fictionalised to a point where few people appreciate where reality stops and fantasy begins; my primary aim has been to show what life was *really* like for the trooper who boiled in the Arizona sun, or froze in the winter Montana winds.

No single volume can cover every facet of such varied service life in exhaustive detail, so it is hoped that this book will serve as a basis upon which the interested reader can build. There are, I am aware, certain areas which the knowledgeable reader will find lacking – officers' clothing has been dealt with only in brief and dress uniforms could not be covered due to the limitations of space.

Those who wish to know more about the battles and the Indians will have to consult one of the many books that cover the subject and readers will find a comprehensive bibliography at the back of this part. I have tried to select books that are readily available, or, in one or two cases, of particular historical significance. To the authors of these books, I can only offer my thanks. For those wishing to visit the sites mentioned, there is a list of excellent museums which capture the flavour of the period.

Many of the photographs are of poor quality due to the early nature of the equipment used; however, they are a vital link with the past, and it is hoped the reader will make allowances for occasional lack of detail.

'A Cavalry troop go on patrol from Fort Bowie, Arizona.' Their neat appearance and universal 1872 forage caps make one wonder if the true reason for the patrol was for the camera. (National Archives)

HISTORICAL BACKGROUND

The period 1865–1890 was one of unparalleled change in American frontier history. This span of 25 years witnessed the end of the traditional nomadic lifestyle of the plains Indians, the colonisation of the West by white settlers, and the first experience of the US Army in fighting a form of irregular warfare at which it did not excel, for which its soldiers and commanders were untrained, and its equipment unsuited. The US Army, both infantry and cavalry, were strangers in a strange land. That they acquitted themselves so well in the face of bureaucratic meddling, poor supply and appalling climatic conditions, speaks highly of the tenacity and physical toughness of the volunteers who served in the West.

Until the return of Lewis and Clark from their expedition in 1806, it was generally accepted by settlers that civilisation stopped west of the Missouri river. Beyond, it was believed there was a land both inhospitable and uninhabitable. Lewis and Clark dispelled this myth, and their accounts of vast mountain ranges, forests and prairies populated by incalculable numbers of animals, did much to fuel the wanderlust of restless immigrants. By the mid-1800s the trickle of western-bound settlers had become a steady stream. The Civil War slowed their procession, but the respite was temporary. From 1865, the trickle again became a flood as war-weary men sought a new life, and this new invasion prompted an increasingly violent backlash from the Indians.

Indian conflicts were, of course, nothing new in American history, from the subjugation of the eastern natives by the first settlers, to the forced resettlement of the Five Civilised Tribes – Cherokee, Choctaw, Chickasaw, Creek and Seminole – in the 1830s. The clash of cultures was to a certain extent inevitable, and exacerbated by white greed and duplicity. In the early 19th century, there were approximately 250,000 Plains Indians living a nomadic and semi-nomadic existence in the sparsely populated West and Mid-west. The West was home to many tribes, the Dakota being the largest, comprising 13 affiliated tribes generically referred to as the Sioux – these included Hunkpapa, Brulé, Oglala, Miniconjou, Sans Arcs and others who shared common language and customs. Other tribes included Nez Percé, Crow, Cheyenne, Comanche and Arapaho, and in the South-west, Navaho and Apache. Their lifestyle was by no means one of peace and tranquillity. Inter-tribal wars flared, raids, ambushes, and theft were commonplace occurrences and hunger and disease were constant companions in lean years.

Tribal life centred around the buffalo, and the importance of this animal in native culture is fundamental in understanding much of the subsequent behaviour of the Indians in their dealings with the white man. From the buffalo, and other wild game, came food, clothing, shelter and raw materials for making everything from combs to weapons. Unlimited access to the plains and its wildlife was vital if the Indian was to remain a free man. Most native culture was based around principles of group loyalty and mutual protection. The idea of property or land ownership was to cause much trouble when government officials introduced ownership treaties. This was a concept utterly alien to the Indian mind, as expressed by Tashunka Witko (Crazy Horse), 'One does not sell the earth upon which the people walk'.

Before and during the Civil War, there had been constant clashes between Plains Indians, settlers and soldiers. In 1862, the Santee Sioux launched a series of attacks in Minnesota. Army action against them served only to further inflame other Dakota tribes, who joined their Santee cousins. By 1865, Wyoming, Nebraska, Kansas, Montana and most of Colorado were suffering from regular Indian depredations. New Mexico, Texas and Arizona were also feeling the wrath of the south-western tribes, but the war in the East soaked up all available men and supplies, leaving the western garrisons starved of everything they required to wage war effectively. With the cessation of hostilities in 1865, fresh demands were made upon the President for help in defeating the rising Indian scourge, demands that could no longer be ignored as westward expansion was being actively encouraged by the Government. In practical terms it was impossible to stop, as the lure of goldfields, trapping, timber and limitless land proved irresistible to the war-weary Easterners. As Indian attacks increased on the wagon trains, miners and settlements, so did the need for military protection. To a great extent the

'Troopers watch for the enemy during the Modoc Wars 1872–3.' Two wear Civil War 'bummer' caps and four-button sack coats. The middle man has his carbine sling and cartridge pouch, the right trooper carries a Sharps carbine. (National Archives)

Major forts and towns of the Indian Wars, 1865–1890.

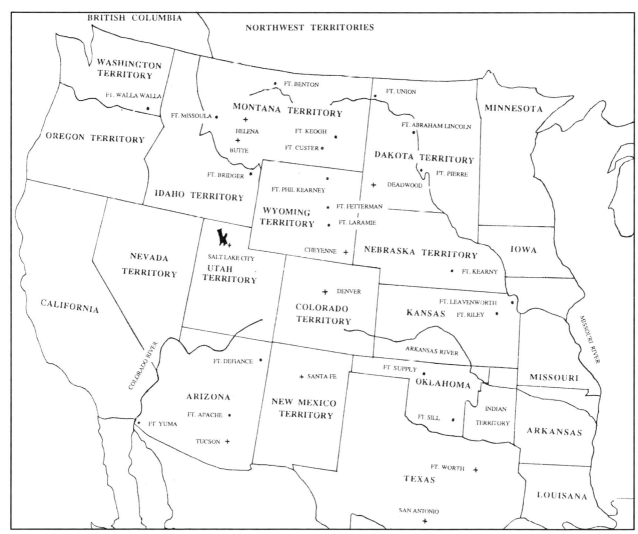

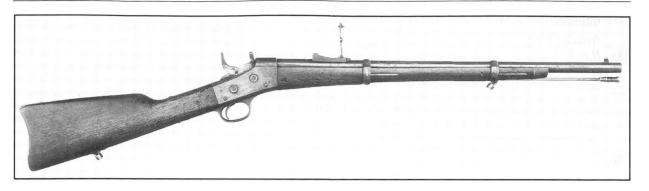

A Remington Rolling-Block carbine in .45-70 calibre. Not as glamorous as a Sharps or Winchester, but a solid, strong weapon that was well liked by those who used it. (Board of Trustees, The Royal Armouries)

Troops in the West were in an impossible situation. They were expected to prevent white encroachment onto reservation land, thus reducing tension with the Indians, whilst at the same time protecting the same whites from physical harm. Over a 25-year period this role changed from peace-keeping to pacification. It became the Army's duty to put Indians on reservations, and ensure they remained there.

There was money to be made in the West and vested interests on the part of Eastern politicians ensured that protection for the mining and lumber camps, trappers and buffalo hunters, would not be long in coming. Two cultures were on a collision course.

CHRONOLOGY

1865 The end of the American Civil War. Assassination of President Lincoln. Appointment of Andrew Johnson as President. Start of operations against the Sioux on the Little Big Horn and Powder Rivers.
The Tongue river fight (Montana).

1866 Gen. W.T. Sherman takes command of the Army in the West. The start of the Snake War.
The Fetterman Massacre (Wyoming), *The battle of Beechers Island* (Colorado), *The fight of Crazy Woman Fork* (Wyoming).

1867 *The Wagon Box fight* (Montana). *The Hayfield fight* (Montana).

1868 Gen. W.T. Sherman appointed General in

Chief. The end of the Snake War.
The battle of the Washita (Oklahoma).

1869 Appointment of Gen. Ulysses Grant as President.
The battle of Summit Springs (Colorado).

1872 Start of the Modoc War.
The fight at Salt River Canyon (Arizona).

1873 *The Lava Bed battles* (California), The end of the Modoc War.
The fight at Massacre Canyon (Nebraska).

1874 The start of Red River War
The fight at Adobe Walls (Texas).
The battles of Tule and Palo Duro Canyons (Texas).

1875 Gen. Crook appointed commander of the Army of the Platte. The end of the Red River War.

1876 The end of the Little Big Horn and Powder River campaign.
The fight of Dull Knife (Wyoming). *The battle of the Rosebud* (Montana). *The battle of Little Big Horn* (Montana).
Death of Chief Crazy Horse (5 September).

1877 Appointment of Rutherford Hayes as President. Start of the Nez Percé and Bannock/Paiute Wars.
The battle of Bear Paw Mountain (Montana). *The fight at Canyon Creek* (Montana). *The fight at the Big Hole* (Montana). *The battle of White Bird Canyon* (Idaho).

1878 *The battle of Willow Springs* (Oregon).
End of the Nez Percé and Bannock/Paiute Wars.

1879 The Ute War.
The Thornburg and Meeker massacres (Colorado).

1881 Appointment of J.A. Garfield as President,

followed by C.A. Arthur. The start of the Apache War.

1882 *Battle of Horseshoe Canyon* (New Mexico). *Battle of Big Dry Wash* (Arizona).

1884 Gen. Sherman succeeded by Gen. P.H. Sheridan as General in Chief.

1885 Appointment of Grover Cleveland as President.

1886 Surrender of Geronimo. End of the Apache War.

1888 Death of Gen. P.H. Sheridan.

1890 Rise of the cult of the Ghost Dance. *The battle of Wounded Knee* (South Dakota). The death of Sitting Bull (15 December). The end of the Indian Wars.

ENLISTMENT

The reasons for enlisting in the Army were almost as many and varied as the number of men who joined. There are few statistics available detailing motives for enlistment, but National Archives records show the average age of a Cavalry trooper was 23 (32 if he was re-enlisting). The background of the men does provide some clues, however. Almost 50 per cent were recent immigrants who joined the Army as a means of obtaining regular pay, an education and a grounding in the English language.

In approximate numerical order, in the ranks of the Cavalry between 1865 and 1890, could be found Irish, German/Austrian, Italian, British, Dutch, French and Swiss, plus a smattering of many other nationalities. Language difficulties were a constant problem, with English-speaking immigrants often translating orders for their compatriots. Poverty, persecution and unemployment were major factors in prompting Europeans to look to America for a new life. The Potato Famine had uprooted 1,000,000 Irishmen, so it was little wonder that the Irish provided the bulk of non-American soldiery. Indeed, of the 260 men who died at Little Big Horn with Custer, approximately 30 per cent were Irish.

Many men, both officers and other ranks, rejoined the Army as a logical continuation of their Civil War service. The long war years had left them mentally unsuited to civilian life, and re-enlistment was their only option. It was these hardened veterans of Cold Harbor, Bull Run and Antietam that provided the post-war Cavalry with the disciplined backbone and experience it needed.

For many young men, the lure of the Cavalry had nothing to do with poverty, homelessness or deprivation. It was simply a case of romanticism overcom-

An oft-used but interesting picture of the 7th Cavalry Gatling Gun left behind by Custer. The man at the left wears a four-button sack coat with added breast pocket. The NCO behind him wears a cut-down 1861 dress frock coat. The soldier right foreground has the later five-button coat, with a homemade 'prairie belt', holding .45-70 ammunition. All are wearing 1872 forage caps. Taken at Fort Lincoln, Dakota, circa 1877. (Little Bighorn Battlefield National Monument)

ing sense. Often those who joined up came from good families and had a trade or professional qualification. Sgt. Frederick Wyllyams, who post-war joined the 7th Cavalry and had served as a volunteer during the Civil War, came from a respectable and wealthy English family, and had been educated at Eton. He was to die at the hands of Sioux warriors.

In his perceptive, contemporary book, *The Story of the Soldier*, Gen. George Forsyth notes a book-keeper, farm boy, dentist, blacksmith, and 'a young man of position' trying to gain a commission, 'a salesman ruined by drink, an Ivory Carver and bowery tough' as trades once enjoyed by an escort party he was accompanying. A company of 7th Cavalry in 1877 held 'a printer, telegraph operator, doctor, two lawyers, three language professors, a harness maker, four cooks and bakers, two black-smiths, a jeweller, three school teachers, as well as farmers, labourers and railroad workers'. Although such a distinguished company was uncommon, some of these professions were well paid and respected, so want was not necessarily the prime cause for their abandonment of civilian life. The desire for a life free of routine drudgery, the chance of open air, adventure and excitement all played their part. $13 a month for privates, rising to $22 for line sergeants, was small incentive for a professional man to join the Cavalry, although it was an improvement on the $2 a week that an unskilled man could earn.

For Negroes, the Army offered more than just an escape from drudgery. It promised social acceptance, a fair wage, chances of promotion, and a sense of racial belonging that few whites could understand.

Discharge after honourable service for a black soldier gave him the chance of better employment and increased social respectability. Black troopers of the 9th and 10th Cavalry consistently proved to be smarter, more reliable and disciplined than comparative white units. Levels of desertion were minimal amongst the black troopers compared to white Cavalry units. They were led by white officers whose loyalty to their black soldiers exhibited a very high degree of commitment, especially in the face of appalling racial prejudice which often led to social ostracism from their contemporaries.

All armies contain a lawless element, and the post-Civil War Cavalry was no exception. Men on the run from family problems, the law or simply at odds with society, would enlist – often under assumed names – and find anonymity in the Army. Some, nicknamed Snowbirds, would sign on to see them through a winter, and then desert, with all their equipment, as soon as the snows melted. Desertion was one of the most serious problems faced by the Government. A report by the adjutant general in 1891 calculated that of 255,712 men who enlisted between 1867 and 1890, 88,475 deserted, a rate of about 33 per cent. In 1867 52 per cent of Custer's 7th Cavalry deserted. This was serious enough in terms of loss of government property, but even more worrying was the inability of the Army, already pared to the bone, to replace the experienced men.

On 28 July 1866, President Johnson made history by signing an Act that actually increased the size of a peacetime regular army. The Cavalry was enlarged from six to ten regiments, each comprising 12

Fort Riley, 1868. The Officers' quarters. One of the more substantial buildings. (Photo T. O'Sullivan. Courtesy J.D. Horan Collection)

Fort Wallace, Kansas, June 1867. The post commander's quarters. The lieutenant standing second right holds a rare Henry repeating rifle. (Yale University Library)

companies, and two regiments (9th and 10th) were composed of black enlisted men. In addition, companies were enlarged from 64 privates to 100. This expansion did not last long in the face of mounting pressure from money-minded congressmen, and on 8 March 1869, the Cavalry were again reduced to 60 privates per company. Between 1874 and 1876 cuts removed commissary and medical staff, company NCOs and cut the number of enlisted men to 54 per company. The Army was thus reduced from 54,000 to 25,000 men.

The shock waves that the massacre of Custer and his men created, again prompted an increase in 1876 to 100 men per Cavalry company, but few were ever able to field more than 50 per cent of their strength at any one time, due to sickness, desertion and post duties. An officer of the 3rd Cavalry stated in 1876 that he had not one officer available to serve with the company on duty. This shortage was to greatly hamper the Army in the West and was indirectly to lead to some serious military reversals.

Officers, too, had their share of problems in the post-war Army. In 1866, the officer corps consisted primarily of West Point graduates and volunteer Civil War veterans, many of whom had been promoted from the ranks – about 12 per cent of the officer total. Post-war promotion and career prospects were dismal for those who stayed on in the regular Army. It would take a 2nd lieutenant about 25 years to reach the rank of major and ten years longer to make colonel.

Ageing senior officers stayed in the Army to receive their pensions, effectively blocking promotion down the line. Many officers took dramatic reduction in rank to retain a regular commission, even to the extent of re-enlisting as a private soldier, as did one ex-Confederate Cavalry major. Pay, compared to professional civilian rates, was also poor, a 2nd lieutenant in the early 1870s earning $115 a month and a colonel $300. The quality of officers varied widely, ranging from the respected and considerate to the alcoholic and reviled, and this standard was reflected to a large extent in the attitude, bearing and efficiency of the battalions and companies under their command and their behaviour in combat.

For any applicant, enlistment was a cursory affair, with a medical check-up on hearing, sight and speech, use of limbs and obvious physical defects. Newly appointed officers may be interviewed by the colonel, or simply given a billet and left to introduce themselves to their fellow officers. Enlisted men were asked to raise their right hand in an oath of allegiance, and, having sworn loyal service to the United States of America, were issued with a basic clothing allowance and despatched to recruit depots for training and eventual allocation to a serving regiment.

TRAINING

For enlisted men in the US Cavalry, the depot at Jefferson Barracks, Missouri, was their only chance to learn the intricacies of military life prior to their despatch to a serving unit. The depot was not, however, a training centre, and none were to exist until the final years of the Indian Wars. The concept of a depot was to provide the recruit with his clothing and equipment allowance, teach him the basics of drill, and keep him busy with fatigues such as guard, stable cleaning or cookhouse duties. No attempt was made to teach weapon handling, horsemanship or tactics. From the 1860s to the late 1870s, even marksmanship was not included in the training programme, and it was left to the whim of the company officers to decide on instruction in that most fundamental of military skills. In 1872, it became a requirement for each man to fire 40 rounds of rifle ammunition, although the regulation was largely ignored. At some posts, ammunition was in such short supply that any form of practice would have left the command almost unable to defend itself in the event of an attack. Lt. E. Godfrey of the 7th Cavalry recalled that his request for target practice with the regimental Gatling gun brought forth the response that he would have to pay for the ammunition himself. The crews never did fire the guns.

It was not until 1879 that a programme was introduced requiring all soldiers to fire 20 rounds per month on a proper range. Up until that date, only the enthusiasm of interested officers enabled troopers to acquire some skill in rifle shooting.

Other basic skills were denied the fledgling troopers. Marching, bivouacking and skirmishing were left to future practical experience, and riding skills were not taught until the recruit joined his regiment. This posed quite a problem as many were from the Eastern states and had no experience whatsoever of horses, and upon assignment to Cavalry regiments proved singularly inept at even mounting a horse, let alone controlling one. When a unit was about to take to the field, this was a serious matter, as shortage of manpower frequently ensured new recruits had to accompany the unit, suffering agonies of saddle soreness in the process. As one officer dryly commented, 'After a good deal of fuss and worry, I got the men mounted ... as may be supposed the sight was as good as a circus and the way several of the men were thrown was a caution.'

The depots served to initiate men swiftly into the ways of army life, teaching them how easy it was to be parted from their money by post traders, unscrupulous NCOs and saloon keepers, and the vagaries of army discipline. Most importantly, it allowed men to establish friendships that were enduring and vital if the lonely and comfortless life on the plains was to be endured. Life at the depots was for most recruits a mixture of routine and boredom, at least until the

Old Fort Hays in 1867. It was as bleak as it looks, and is an excellent example of the typical condition of most early forts. (Kansas State Historical Society)

Cavalrymen at rifle practice. Each man seems to have adopted a different method of wearing his hat. The trooper in the foreground holds a Trapdoor Springfield carbine and wears a carbine sling and webbing cartridge belt. (National Archives)

army reorganisations of the late 1880s, when proper training procedures were established, and spare time became jealously guarded in between small arms drill, physical exercises, close order marching and lectures on care and usage of weapons and equipment. Cavalry recruits at Jefferson Barracks had in addition mounted and dismounted sabre drill (even though by this date the sabre had ceased to be of any practical use in combat), equitation and target practice.

Early on in the post-war period, few recruits could expect to stay for long at a depot, as manpower was too short. Some stayed only a few days, others a few weeks, depending on the needs of their assigned regiments. Reaching those regiments was, for many, an adventure in itself. Railroad accommodation of the most basic type was used wherever possible, usually with no provision for toilets or proper food, but to the excited enlisted men, it was an adventure into the unknown. They forayed for food at every possible opportunity, shot at game, begged for hot water from the engineers, and cooked meals on the wagon floors. At the end of the line at Dakota or Wyoming, if they were lucky transferred to horse-drawn wagons, waiting to carry them still further west. If not they walked, as one draft did after leaving the railhead at

Corinne, Utah. A month later they arrived at their post in Helena, Montana, 600 miles away. Once at his post, the trooper was assigned to a company in which he would stay for his entire subsequent army career, accepting as friends or enemies, the men, NCOs and officers who comprised that company.

UNIFORM AND EQUIPMENT

The lure of the military uniform has long been a strong one for many young men, but in practical terms the uniform of the Civil War Cavalry was as unsuitable as any uniform could be for the rigours of field service. This unsuitability was compounded by the reluctance of Congress and the Army to approve any expenditure over and above what was absolutely necessary. The novice cavalryman of 1866–1872 was issued with civil war surplus uniform, familiar to any volunteer of pre-1861. At the outset, it should be stressed that the campaign cavalryman, in the years 1865–1880, bore little or no relationship to the grey-hatted, yellow-striped and neckerchiefed image of the Hollywood fantasy. In fact, considerable latitude

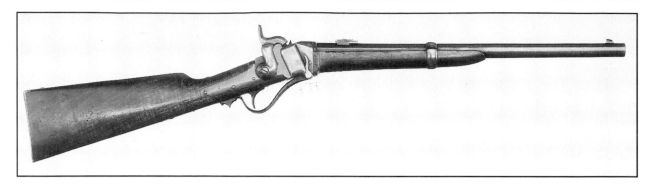

A percussion, slant-breech Sharps carbine, .52 calibre. A popular rifle with both cavalry and indians. (Board of Trustees, The Royal Armouries)

was allowed in personal clothing and equipment, mainly through sheer necessity. Issue clothing was often so poor it disintegrated, and civilian manufactured clothing was usually better made, more durable and comfortable. As Charles King, 5th Cavalry, noted, when issued with field orders, '...we had fallen back on our comfortable old Arizona scouting suits, and were attired in deerskin, buckskin, flannels and corduroy ... you could not have told officer from private'. No account was taken of the climatic conditions in which the soldier was to serve, which on the plains would vary from $-40\,°F$ in winter to $120\,°F$ in summer. Regardless, the same clothing was issued.

This consisted of the sack coat, a loose collared hip-length jacket made of a coarse, dark blue, woven wool, with four brass buttons. The old style shell jacket, a waist-length, close-fitting, high-collared coat could also be found in service, and post-war was still preferred by many long-serving regulars as smarter and more military than the sack coat. A grey or blue flannel shirt was also issued, which was almost invariably replaced by more comfortable civilian patterns – some button fronted, others with three or four buttons at the neck and, particularly popular, the 'fireman's' shirt, with a buttoned flap across the chest. A set of long woollen underwear which itched furiously in hot weather was also supplied.

The issue trousers were of sky blue Kersey wool, with plain metal buttons for use with white woven cotton braces. The trousers were not up to the demands of days in contact with a saddle, and wore out at the seat and inner thighs rapidly. The usual remedy was to reinforce them with white canvas where it was available, otherwise burlap sacks or meal bags would be used. Some idea of the state of campaigning troopers can be gained from the comments of Sgt. John Ryan, whose men after a winter campaign in 1868 were '...almost destitute of clothing, our trousers being patched with seamless meal bags. A large number of the hats belonging to men were made of the same material. The legs of our cavalry boots were pretty scorched and burned from standing around camp fires and as substitutes we used leggings made from pieces of tents. A number of men had to use woollen blankets in place of overcoats.'

For privates, trousers were often issued without the distinctive $\frac{1}{8}$ in. wide yellow stripe denoting cavalry service, and up to 1872, many cavalrymen, including NCOs, could be found wearing completely plain, unpiped blue trousers. Post-1872, regulations required officers to wear a $1\frac{1}{2}$ in. stripe, sergeants 1 in. and corporals $\frac{1}{2}$ in. Such regulations were not necessarily obeyed, and often the situation continued much as before, with soldiers wearing what was available at the time.

Headgear was either a 'Hardee' or 'Jeff Davis' black felt hat with a flat crown and turned-up brim around which was a yellow branch-of-service cord, or a Civil War fatigue hat or 'bummer'; a rather shapeless version of the peaked French Army Kepi. The Kepi stayed in use for a surprising length of time considering its impracticality, as one soldier caustically commented, a clam shell would have been about as useful.

A broad-brimmed hat was by far the most practical on campaign. More than any other single item of clothing, headgear expressed the individuality of the cavalryman. Civilian hats of every colour and shape abounded, with straw hats proving particularly popular amongst both enlisted men and officers. '. . . in the field, we see no forage caps, but in their stead hats, white hats, brown hats, black hats, all kind of hats except the service hat, for that too is unsuitable.'

Footwear was always a contentious issue in the Army. During the war, the majority of cavalry troopers wore the ankle-length shoe or bootee. Their over-long trousers generally permitted the hem to rest over the shoe when mounted, although when walking the trouser bottoms would drag on the ground and looked unsightly. Boots were preferred by those who could obtain them, and in the latter years of the war, the high cavalry boot became more generally available. It was square toed, the left and right being indistinguishable, with either a small cuban or flat leather heel, of sewn or pegged construction, with the back $15\frac{1}{2}$ ins. high, ending just at the top of the calf, whilst the front was 4 ins. higher, arching up to cover the knee when the wearer was in the saddle. There was a preference on the part of the quartermaster general to order sewn boots, as wartime boots which were pegged (the uppers held to the soles by brass screws) had proved deficient in service. The black calfskin or grain leather uppers on the Cavalry boot were thin by modern standards, and as issued the government footwear was not renowned for its longevity. The uppers parted from the soles, the heels were easily ripped off and if much walking was required, the soles could wear through in a month. Cpl. Reed, 4th Mounted Infantry, stated that after a forced march in the autumn of 1867, he and his men '. . . staggered into Fort Laramie, that is, what was left of us, our feet wrapped in our torn blankets, as our shoes were gone'.

Many methods were adopted to break in new boots including soaking them, and then drying them on the feet, or coating feet and socks with soap, both of which achieved satisfactory results. Others bought custom-made boots. Cpl. Jacob Horner, 7th Cavalry, purchased a pair of beautiful handmade boots from his company captain, noting, 'almost every soldier in the post borrowed my boots and was photographed wearing them'.

With the boot, a brass-bodied rowel spur was routinely worn, although some enlisted men and officers purchased fancy spurs often made of Mexican silver with eagle heads and other ornate designs.

Officers' uniforms

The situation for officers was less dire where clothing was concerned. Most had their uniforms modified to fit by regimental tailors, or simply purchased better quality items from civilian suppliers. Some, and Col. George Custer was a splendid example, designed uniforms to their own taste, and had them made to order. There was virtually no item of uniform that could not be privately purchased, and on campaign most officers were as unmilitary a spectacle as their men. Gen. Crook was renowned for his campaign dress of either a straw hat or pith helmet, cotton jacket over a civilian shirt, and breeches tucked into riding boots. Many learned quickly about the practicalities of adopting Indian dress, and probably more than any other article of clothing, buckskin became almost obligatory on the plains. Buckskin jackets, trousers and leggings were almost indestructible, and in wet weather the fringes permitted the sodden leather to drain quickly, as each fringe became a soakaway. Headgear was as varied as that of the enlisted men, with straw boaters being particularly popular, and boots, such as those bought by Cpl. Horner from his captain, were usually civilian-made. More latitude was permitted with regards to officers' footwear: many sported knee-high boots with turned-over tops, whilst others preferred boots which came to just below the knee. Canvas and buckskin leggings would also be worn where circumstances required.

Leather accoutrements in their basic form changed little over the Indian Wars period, and much that was wartime issue continued to be in use until the

An issue Cavalry belt buckle, in brass with silver wreath. This specimen was found on the Rosebud battlefield in 1896. (Author's collection)

A troop of the 6th Cavalry waiting to hit the trail, Arizona, 1880. (National Archives)

Army reforms of the late 1880s. The standard issue, early sabre belt comprised a black or buff leather belt, between 1½ ins. and 2 ins. wide, with the old oval dragoon 'US' belt plate in brass, or more commonly the 1851 regulation rectangular plate with a silver wreath of laurel leaves encircling the Arms of the United States, comprising an eagle, shield and scroll with the motto *E Pluribus Unum*. There were two leather suspension straps for the sabre, and a single shoulder strap. Elsewhere on the belt would be hung a leather holster closed with a flap, cap box containing percussion caps, pistol cartridge pouch, and carbine cartridge pouch. The carbine was hung on a broad, black leather sling carried over the left shoulder, and when mounted, the muzzle of the gun would be inserted in a round leather socket to the rear of the right leg. As with all of the equipment in use in this period, there was a bewildering number of types and variations. The model 1855 cap pouch, 1855 Infantry cartridge box, model 1861 pistol cartridge pouch, 1874 Dyer pouch and pattern 1872 Infantry cartridge boxes all gradually found their way into service, along with many home-produced items. Possibly the most important modification was the adoption of the looped 'Prairie Belt', possibly first introduced in 1866 by Capt. Anson Mills. It was an issue, or civilian made, leather belt with hand-stitched leather loops on it to contain cartridges. It was both comfortable to wear, as the weight was more evenly distributed, and practical, as it could contain far more cartridges than

a pouch. In 1867, Col. Hazen introduced a removable looped pouch which found some favour.

Most cavalrymen used some form of gloves when on campaign, usually a short gauntlet style, made of buckskin, tanned leather or in exceptionally cold weather, muskrat, beaver or sealskin. The requirements of ill-equipped troopers in the deadly Western winters was a considerable problem. No allowance was made by the clothing bureau for the seasons apart from the provision of a caped sky-blue greatcoat, until the uniform changes of 1872, so most field soldiers and officers who endured winter conditions utilised what was readily to hand, and adopted buffalo-skin coats, trousers and overshoes (these were usually liberally stuffed with straw). Buffalo or beaverskin hats with earflaps protected the head while fur mitts gave the hands some protection. Their appearance must certainly have been bizarre, as Alice Baldwin, wife of a Cavalry officer stationed in Dakota, recounted. 'Clad in Buffalo skins, trousers and overcoat with the fur inside, mufflers over his ears, hands encased in fur mittens, his face in a mask leaving space sufficient only to see his way, he presents an appearance rivalling his Eskimo brother.'

It is curious to note that whilst in contemporary literature cavalrymen appeared to accept the heat as an inevitable part of campaign life, the cold was regarded by most troopers with the utmost fear. As they were often lacking suitable clothing, sudden storms could quickly kill or maim. In an article written many years later on his experiences, Gen. E. J. McClemand recalled such a snowstorm in Montana, reducing troopers to such a state that 'they wept and begged to be permitted to lie down and die

... for a time it looked as though all discipline would be lost'.

In 1872, the War Department made some attempt to improve the type and quality of clothing issued. These changes were made not so much out of a desire to improve the lot of the soldier, but as sheer necessity brought about by shortage of the popular sizes of Civil War surplus uniform. Many contractors had maximised profits during the war by producing drastically undersized uniforms, which when issued proved too small to fit even the most diminutive trooper. Nevertheless, wartime manufactured clothing was still being issued as late as 1880. It was appreciated by all that the old uniform was ill fitting, unsoldierly and in many instances impractical. The 'Bummer' cap was redesigned to be neater, and a black felt campaign hat was introduced. It was very broad brimmed with an indented crown, with the novel facility of being able to hook up the brim so that it resembled a Napoleonic cocked hat. Col. D.S. Stanley called it 'the most useless uncouth rag ever put on a man's head'. In wet weather it drooped hopelessly and lost all shape, and fell apart in a few weeks on campaign. A similar pattern was introduced in 1875 but was little better, and it was not until the introduction of the tan-coloured 1885 campaign hat that some semblance of practical headgear began to appear.

If the cavalryman had cause to grumble over the quality of uniforms issued to him prior to 1872, his mood was hardly lightened by the appearance of the 1872 pleated fatigue blouse. This ill-conceived jacket had nine buttons, and four wide pleats each side. It soon lost its creases, the seams attracted vermin on campaign and the cavalrymen hated it. It was withdrawn in 1874 and replaced by a five-button sack coat of similar type to the Civil War issue, but with yellow collar piping and a more shaped cut. The style lasted through to the end of the Indian Wars, being slightly modified in 1883 with the omission of the branch-of-service piping. Slight alterations were made to the trousers, not the least important being the order that all mounted troops should have reinforced seats!

There were many other minor changes in accoutrements. The sabre belt was provided with adjustable brass sliders for sabre straps, instead of the old fixed 'D' rings, and the straps themselves were no longer stud fastened to the sliders, but had brass hooks, making it easier to hang the sabre from the saddle mounts. The holster was modified, with the size of the top flap reduced and the body of the holster less shaped. In 1876 the Ordnance Department began manufacturing 'prairie belts' with canvas loops stitched onto a leather backing. These were an

Soldiers and Apache scouts during the war against Geronimo. Note all three standing troopers carry pistols in open civilian style holsters. Fumbling to open a flap holster could mean the difference between life and death. (Arizona Historical Society)

improvement over the cartridge boxes, but it wasn't until 1881 that the Mills webbing cartridge belt was adopted.

The horse

Often ignored, and frequently abused, it was the horse that provided the vital motive force for both sides during the wars of 1865–90. Indian mastery of their animals was legendary. Trained in warfare and horsemanship from boyhood, warriors were at one with their mounts. The Indian pony was a hardier breed than the Government animals, with greater stamina, as Albert Barnitz noted in his diary in June 1867, '[The Indians] were usually mounted on ponies ... the ponies were, however, of remarkable size, and very fleet and powerful. Our own horses were generally no match for them, either in speed or endurance.' However, the Indians' grass-fed animals were incapable of sustained winter use, which did not hamper the US animals, provided supplies of grain were available. The Indian practice of riding bareback, or with a thin wooden and blanket saddle, was, however, not one that caught on in the US Army!

From 1858 to the end of the wars, the McClellan saddle was used in a number of modified forms. It comprised a wooden base, or tree, with a long oval cut-out running almost the entire length to permit passage of air, and prevent sweating and chaffing. It had a raked cantle low pommel, and had its edges and strap slots covered with brass. Initially the saddle was plain rawhide covered, with leather side skirts, but this was prone to shrinkage and splitting in the rain and sun of the prairie, and quickly rendered the saddle useless. Subsequent to trials in 1870, saddles were produced covered in undyed or black leather. In 1874 it was recommended that all saddles be covered in black leather. The McClellan equipment had its faults. The curb bit, bridle, halter and link were complex, whilst the stirrups, covered by distinctive leather hoods, required considerable improvement. Designed to protect the rider from cold and thick brush, they tended to trap the foot, whilst enabling rust to form on the stirrup platform leading to subsequent disintegration of the whole stirrup. Worse still was the lack of breast strap to prevent the saddle from sliding backwards, particularly when ascending hills, when the blanket could work out from underneath the saddle. Generally, two years was the maximum service life of the McClellan.

The Army Board of July 1879 recommended that a cavalryman carry the following: one saddle tree, leather covered, two stirrup straps, five coat straps, one head-stall, one pair of reins, one felt saddle cloth,

one surcingle, one side line, one lariat, one horse brush, one carbine loop, one carbine socket and strap, one hair girth, one bit, one curb and strap, one blanket, one link, one nosebag, one picket pin, one curry comb. In addition to this, troopers stowed personal effects and mess gear – skillet, eating utensils, spare socks and shirt – in leather saddlebags carried behind the saddle. His blanket was carried rolled on the front of his saddle; greatcoat and, in hot weather, his tunic, at the rear. The round, felt-covered tin canteen was hung over the saddle pommel with the vital tin coffee cup firmly attached to any handy strap.

The mounting rings for the sabre enabled it to be suspended from the left side of the saddle. The scabbard curved back under the rider's leg, leaving the grip of the sabre within easy reach of the right hand. The lariat was usually tied to the saddle on the same side, acting as a cushion between the sword and horse. A nosebag was hung from a ring on the front right of the saddle, close to the pommel, so that it rested slightly forward of the rider's right knee. Adding the weight of a trooper, each horse was carrying around 250 lbs, and, thus equipped, the cavalryman was ready for the field.

WEAPONS

If the Cavalry trooper was inferior to the Indian in horsemanship and natural fighting ability, he was certainly superior in respect of his firepower.

In 1870 there was still a complete lack of standardisation in weaponry carried by Cavalry regiments. Approximately 25 per cent of units were equipped with the Sharps carbine, the rest had a mixture of Spencers, Springfields, Remington rolling-blocks, plus a smattering of other rifles such as Burnsides or Henry's. Pistols comprised a mixture of Colt Army & Navy and Remington Army revolvers. The only universally issued weapon was the pattern 1860 Cavalry sabre. It was a situation that demanded some regularisation if supply was not to degenerate into total confusion.

There was little doubt in the minds of soldiers who had combat experience that the muzzle loading rifle musket had been superseded by the metallic cartridge rifle. The issue of the Spencer, a seven-shot, magazine-fed rifle, had transformed the battlefield, although it was a transformation that went largely unnoticed. A man no longer had to expose himself to enemy fire whilst he stood up to reload a musket – a cartridge weapon could be loaded and fired from the prone position. In the case of the Spencer, its repeating fire capability meant that its users, provided with suitable cover and a good ammunition

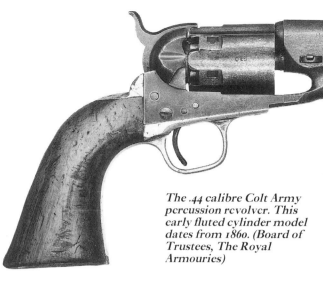

The .44 calibre Colt Army percussion revolver. This early fluted cylinder model dates from 1860. (Board of Trustees, The Royal Armouries)

supply, were almost unassailable. The 7th Cavalry had shown this in 1868 during the Battle of the Washita, when a vastly superior Indian force were driven back by the unrelenting fire of the regiment's Spencers.

The rimfire .52 calibre Spencer had its shortcomings. The cartridge was underpowered, a constant problem with rimfires, and its effective range was about 300 yards, although it was capable in the hands of a good shot, of killing at far greater distances. If the carbine was dropped, the cartridges in the tubular magazine, housed in the butt, were prone to self-detonation. The Blakeslee cartridge box, containing ten magazine tubes, gave a trooper 70 rounds of ammunition, which could be fired accurately at a rate of ten rounds per minute, about five times the rate of fire of a musket. Only a few units were equipped with the Blakeslee box though, and the rest carried their cartridges in a pouch, their copper casing vulnerable to damage, making them difficult to load, and sometimes impossible to extract. For that reason a lot of troopers preferred the slower reliability of the .52 calibre percussion Sharps, as is well illustrated by Maj. C. Hardin, '. . . a certain troop, 1st Cavalry, armed with Spencers, went into action with a bad lot of rimfire cartridges. Several men of that troop told me that the failure of so many cartridges almost caused a panic, and would have caused a panic had it not been for the fact that other troops with them had Sharps carbines that never missed fire.'

By the early 1870s, the Sharps was already a venerable veteran of the frontier, the falling block

action having been introduced in 1859. Originally using a .52 calibre linen cartridge, it was a strong, reliable weapon with a rate of fire about half that of the Spencer, and its ability to take abuse made it popular with the troops who used it. In 1870, at the suggestion of the Board of Ordnance, remaining stocks of Sharps rifles were converted to use the .50-70 Springfield centrefire cartridge. (.50 in. calibre, using 70 grains of black powder. Carbines used a reduced charge of 45 grains and a lighter bullet.) This modification eliminated two of the major weaknesses of the old linen cartridge, flash from the gap between the block and chamber, caused by loose powder and escaping gas, and fouling of the chamber by powder residue after several rounds had been discharged.

A quantity of muzzle-loading Springfield rifles and carbines had been converted by means of the Allin system into breech loaders, using the .50-70 centrefire cartridge. The Army were not happy with the performance of the .50-70 cartridge and the lack of standardisation, so in late 1872, a board was convened in New York to look into adopting a breech-loading system. A number of weapons were tested – Spencer, Sharps, Remington, Springfield, Winchester, as well as the British Snider, and Callisher and Terry carbines. The eventual winner was the Allin Springfield, with the recommendation of a reduction in calibre to .45 in., and for carbine use a reduction in charge from 70 to 55 grains.

For the cavalrymen using the rifle, this was of considerable importance, for the recoil was punishing enough with the reduced charge, as shown by the comments of 7th Cavalryman, C.H. Allen. When target shooting, the men 'had sockets to put over the butts of the carbine and on top of that we were glad to put paper or anything we could get to keep it from the shoulder. I was black and blue all over the shoulder and down into my chest.' For a joke, a man might substitute a full .45-70 rifle cartridge in place of the .45-55. One trooper recalled that firing it from a carbine '. . . you thought the sky fell in'.

With small modifications, the Model 1873 Springfield usually referred to as the 'Trap-Door' – remained in Cavalry service until the adoption of the Krag Jorgensen bolt-action rifle in the 1890s. Most officers chose to carry a sporting rifle version of the Springfield (often engraved and with target sights), since the ammunition was easy to obtain and the performance of the rifle acceptable. It had a flatter trajectory and a greater effective range than the .50-70, though it was arguably more accurate than the men who fired it, as the standard of marksmanship was generally very poor among both officers and enlisted men.

Pistols

Of increasing popularity was the pistol, which had become a necessity for the cavalryman during the Civil War. At the close quarters that most Cavalry engagements were fought the revolver could outreach the sabre and outgun carbines, which required reloading after each shot, and in desperate straits the butt of a pistol made a handy club. Up to 1873, a number of revolvers were used in the Cavalry. The most solidly constructed was the Remington New Model .44, a solid framed six-shot percussion model, which could take a lot of misuse and clumsy handling without breaking. One of the drawbacks of the early Remingtons was the ease with which the axis pin (which retained the cylinder in the pistol) could be lost, instantly rendering the gun useless. Later models were modified to prevent this and the Remington was widely used in the West. Used in even greater numbers were Colt's Army and Navy revolvers in .44 and .36 calibre respectively. Of open-topped construction, they were reliable in service but very prone to frame damage because of the lack of a strengthening bar over the cylinder. If used as a club, the barrel could end up an inch out of true. The Colts saw much service in the Civil War and post-war cavalrymen carried them out of sentimental value as much as anything. Other revolvers abounded and Le Mat, Starr and multi-barrelled pepperbox pistols were also used. One disadvantage of the percussion pistols was their need to be kept dry to prevent

powder and caps from becoming waterlogged. They were also prone to multiple ignition as the flash from one chamber ignited all the others, as was clearly demonstrated by the experience of Chaplain White, 2nd Cavalry, who had been caught in an ambush by Sioux Indians in July 1866. Armed with a huge, seven-barrelled English pepperbox pistol, he fired as several Indians leaped into the ravine he was sheltering in. All seven charges ignited simultaneously, killing one Indian and frightening the others so much that they fled. The experience presumably did little to soothe the Chaplain's nerves.

Clearly, some rationalisation was required, especially as the advent of more reliable metallic cartridges meant that rimfire and particularly centre-fire revolvers were becoming more practical. A number of weapons were examined by the Board of Ordnance through 1871–72, Smith and Wesson, Remington, Colt, Webley and Tranter revolvers were tested. Probably for the sake of mechanical simplicity, the Board favoured single rather than double-action, and the selection was the .45 calibre Model 1872 Colt. Some percussion Colts had been converted under the Richards patent to use rimfire cartridges and it was clear that the future lay with cartridge, not percussion weapons. Prior to the adoption of the metallic cartridge, the fragile paper-wrapped cartridges for use in the percussion pistols were carried loose in pouches. The constant vibration of riding caused rapid disintegration of the paper and wise troopers carried a flask of black powder, or spare, loaded, revolver cylinders. Capt. F. Benteen, 'H' Co. 7th Cavalry, commented in a report on ordnance on 12 March 1874 that 'In my opinion, the purchase of ammunition for pistols used by the Cavalry should be

Troopers of Crooks' expedition of 1876 butcher a horse. (Denver Public Library)

confined wholly to metallic cartridges, all paper cartridges being wasted by being jolted to pieces in the pouch'.

Colt had produced an open-topped .44 calibre rimfire revolver in 1872, which resembled the early percussion Army revolver, but its modification to a solid framed .45 calibre centrefire pistol in 1873 was sufficient to sway the Board of Ordnance. An order for 8,000 Model 1873 Army revolvers with $7\frac{1}{2}$ in. barrels was placed in late 1873, and supplies began to trickle into service early the following year. The use of metallic cartridges created a new set of problems for the cavalryman, aside from the usual problem of distortion in the pouch. The increasingly frequent use of prairie belts of looped leather in the humidity of the Western plains created verdigris which, if not removed before a cartridge was fired, could turn into a solid cement with the heat of discharge, rendering ejection impossible. Surviving weapons examined after the Custer débâcle, showed evidence of jammed cases, their bases having been ripped off by the ejector mechanism. Additionally, it should be remembered that black powder fouling could exacerbate the problem, especially in very dusty conditions. The problem was partially alleviated in 1881 with the adoption of the webbing cartridge belt, but was never entirely resolved.

The single-action Colt became the most instantly recognisable revolver in the world, mainly because of the enthusiasm of Hollywood film producers for representing it as the only pistol ever carried by the US Cavalry. This, of course, was not so; although 37,000 were issued to the Army between 1873 and 1891, other revolvers were also supplied. The top-break .44 in. Smith and Wesson 1869 and .45 in. Schofield Smith and Wesson of 1875 were issued to Cavalry and infantry units, as well as a limited number of Model 1875 Remington Army revolvers. Cavalrymen liked the hard-hitting and accurate revolvers, which in a tight situation were often the difference between life and death, as Albert Barnitz recounts. Having shot two braves at close quarters with his pistol, he was faced with a warrior on foot armed with a large-bore Lancaster rifle. The Indian dodged from one side of Barnitz's horse to the other eventually jumping out and firing at near point-blank range at the same instant as Barnitz who said 'Mine [bullet] I believe must have passed through his heart as he threw his hands up frantically and ... died almost immediately'.

Knives

A vital, though unofficial piece of equipment for every cavalryman was his knife. They varied hugely in type and pattern, though the most popular were the 'Bowie' style with a single-edged, clipped point blade and grips that varied from plain wood to silver-mounted ivory. A large number of Sheffield-made

A bivouac for men on Crooks' 'starvation march'. No proper tents were issued so blankets over a frame of saplings had to suffice. (Denver Public Library)

Gen. Crook in campaign dress, with two Apache scouts, 1881. He preferred to carry a short-barrelled shotgun to the issue Springfield. (Arizona Historical Society Library)

knives were imported and proved very durable. Some cavalrymen carried their knives in plain leather scabbards, but a lot of men liked the decorated, fringed buckskin sheaths worn by the Indians, and many photographs show them prominently displayed on the sabre belt. The knives were used for skinning and butchering game, opening tins, and occasionally taking scalps. During the desperate defence of their ridge, 7th Cavalrymen under Capt. Benteen used their knives to dig shallow rifle pits to give greater protection from hostile fire. It was not until 1880 that the Army acknowledged the need for a serviceable knife and introduced a Springfield-manufactured double-edged hunting knife, with an $8\frac{1}{2}$ in. blade, brass mounts and rounded wooden handle.

Some cavalrymen provided weapons at their own expense. Private Tuttle of the 7th Cavalry, an excellent shot, used a sporting Springfield rifle to kill Sioux warriors at ranges beyond that of the carbine. Most troopers admired the repeating Winchester rifle, which had been in existence since 1865, when it was made as a rimfire and sold as the Henry. However, the Army's dislike of multi-shot rifles meant that the troops were often faced with Indians using Winchesters or Spencers whilst they were armed only with the single-shot Springfield. A considerable amount of literature has been devoted to the subject of Indian firearms. Generally, they were not as well armed as the troopers, and many of their weapons were in a poor mechanical state. The Indians also had difficulty in obtaining the right ammunition and frequently used incorrect and incompatible cartridges.

The sabre

The most instantly recognisable symbol of the cavalryman was the sabre. It was this weapon that led to the Indian describing troopers as 'long knives' and in close combat it could prove a formidable weapon. Lt. Grummond, 2nd Cavalry, had cause to use his sabre in earnest when ambushed in the Peno Valley, Wyoming, in December 1866. Pursued by Indians intent on pulling the soldiers from their mounts, Grummond '...abandoned the use of spurs and jammed his sword into the weary beast to urge him to greater effort, followed by a Chief in full war dress with spear at his back so near that but for his good horse he would then and there met a terrible fate'. Grummond recounted that 'he shut his eyes and literally slashed his way out, as did many of the others, recalling that he heard his sabre click every time he cleaved an Indian's skull'.

A year later, Capt. A. Barnitz, 7th Cavalry, quoted another instance of its use during an action near Fort Wallace on 26 June 1867. 'A Chief mounted on a white horse ... was killed by Cpl. Harris, who

An officer and scouts during the Apache wars. The white scout wears buckskins and carries a Winchester, whilst one Apache has adopted a spiked dress helmet! The officer wears a regulation jacket, civilian slouch hat, buckskin trousers and boots. (Arizona Historical Society Library)

first engaged him with a sabre as he was attempting to plunge a lance through Private Hardiman (whose carbine was empty and whose sabre had unfortunately become disengaged from the scabbard in the pursuit and been lost).' Such accounts exaggerate the use of the sabre, however, as most troopers would prefer to place their trust in a firearm, and keep as much distance as possible between themselves and the Indians, whose prowess with club, lance and bow was exceptional.

The Model 1860 Light Cavalry Sabre was a lighter and less unwieldly version of the heavy Cavalry sabre of 1840, which had been modelled on the French 1822 pattern sabre. The Model 1840 was dubbed 'Old Wristbreaker' and demanded considerable strength and expertise to wield. The Model 1860 was of very similar appearance, but of lighter construction and less blade-heavy. It weighed 3 lbs 7 oz and measured $41\frac{1}{2}$ ins. overall with a $34\frac{5}{8}$ in. curved single-edged blade, wire-wrapped grip and three-bar, brass guard. Some officers elected to carry the standard Model 1860, but most chose an officer's pattern, which was of similar appearance, having a gilded brass hilt with decorative oakleaves. The steel scabbard was blued, as opposed to the browned ones of the enlisted men.

Times had changed on the plains since the introduction of the 1840 sabre. Indians had ceased to do battle armed only with lances, bows and tomahawks. By the end of the war, a large proportion of warriors (possibly as many as 80 per cent) had some

form of firearm, ranging from early flintlock pistols to the latest Winchesters and Sharps rifles. Close combat of the type described by Barnitz became less frequent as the years passed. The sabre was cumbersome and noisy to carry, and was rarely sharp enough to cut a cooked piece of meat, let alone hack through a buffalo hide shield. Indeed, the sabres were issued blunt, and few armourers possessed any means of sharpening them. Sabre practice was almost unknown until the end of the 1870s, by which time it had been well and truly eclipsed by the firearm. On campaign most commanders ordered the swords to be packed and left behind, and from 1870 onwards, it became rare to see a cavalry regiment in the field wearing them. Prior to the Little Big Horn, Custer ordered all sabres to be put into store, and the 7th went into action with only one sabre worn by an officer, Lt. De Rudio, who never unsheathed it during the combat. Despite claims after the battle that Custer and his men would have survived had they carried swords, there is no evidence to support the fact. A sabre is no use in the face of firearms and arrows. The Indians regarded captured sabres as prized trophies, and appeared to use them in combat with considerable enthusiasm.

Nevertheless, despite heated debate, the sabre remained in service in one form or another until the end of the First World War. Not until 18 April 1934 was an order published declaring 'the sabre is hereby discontinued as an item of issue to the Cavalry. The sabre is completely discarded as a cavalry weapon.'

FIELD SERVICE

Arrival at a remote post was usually something of a shock for the new cavalryman. After long cramped train journeys, the troopers would transfer to wagons, or march to their ultimate destination. Some were able to travel by river steamer, but all were tired, dirty and hungry upon their arrival. For the earliest reinforcements, after the cessation of hostilities in 1865, there were no forts to welcome them. Fort Reno on the Powder River in Montana, Fort Phil Kearney in Dakota territory in Wyoming and a string of other isolated outposts were built by the soldiers who were to garrison them. Most early Western forts were of earth, sod and wood construction, with adobe or brick additions as time and availability permitted. They provided the most basic protection, but were home to numerous insects. They leaked in the wet and froze in winter, and lumps of earth constantly dropped upon the inmates. At their most basic, they comprised an officers' quarters, barracks, guard room, sick bay, and workshop protected by a wooden stockade with one or more guard towers. By the 1880s, the permanent forts had blossomed into solidly constructed sites often occupying several acres, and numbering such amenities as canteens, reading rooms, chapel, married quarters, hospital and workshops. The beaten earth floors gave way to timber, and barracks were equipped with wooden arms racks, steel framed beds, clothing and personal effects lockers and iron stoves. It was at least better than their accommodation in the field. Cavalrymen travelled light, carrying only a rubberised poncho or extra blanket to act as makeshift tents. Charles King recalled their misery in a torrential downpour, 'We built "wickyups" of saplings and elastic twigs, threw ponchos and blankets over them and crawled under, but 'twas no use, the whole country was flooded ... and we huddled round them in the squashy mud.'

Fatigue duties were a common curse for all soldiers, and none more so than for the men in outlying garrisons in the middle of hostile territory. Many forts were sited to maximise the ease with which they could be defended with amenities coming second to military necessity. Water, wood and hay-cutting parties were sent out only under armed guard. Even so, they were tempting targets for lightning attacks by hostile bands, and some of the subsequent pitched battles achieved almost legendary status, such as the Hayfield and Wagon Box fights near Forts C.F. Smith and Phil Kearney on 1 and 2 August 1867, when large parties of Sioux and Cheyennes, under Chief Red Cloud, tried and failed to overrun working parties. Other fatigue parties were not so lucky, and search parties often stumbled across their bodies, as a trooper from the 2nd Cavalry recorded. When looking for water near Crazy Woman Creek in Wyoming, they found the dead body of a white man, scalped and mutilated. Remains of a grey shirt still on the shoulders indicated he had probably been a soldier. 'The finding of the dead body ... had a very depressing effect on the entire command.'

Adjusting to their new circumstances was not easy for the cavalrymen. There was no relief from the routine of post life unless the regiment embarked on a campaign, and there was nowhere to go when off duty, the nearest towns often being two or three days' journey away. At new forts, soldiers would be constantly working as labourers, giving rise to the posts being nicknamed 'Government Workhouses'. For recreation, men particularly enjoyed sports, which could include such delights as baseball, horse racing, greased pig wrestling, a greased pole climb, sack, wheelbarrow, and three-legged races as well as more traditional foot races and tug-of-war. Winners could receive useful cash prizes and competition was intense; the exercise relieved tension and promoted team spirit.

When available, alcohol was a favourite means of relaxation and was the cause of more disciplinary trouble than any other single factor. Weak beer was usually available, but no liquor could be purchased at posts in reservation land, so substitutes were concocted by desperate soldiers. Some were poisonous, such as grain alcohol and Jamaica Ginger, and could cause blindness, spasms and death. In the south-west, a popular drink was Mescal, a cactus alcohol. One cavalryman who drank it recounted he had to be tied up for two days afterwards and never drank again in his life. Most alcohol was purchased from passing traders or sutlers, civilian traders permitted to sell goods at Army posts. In the late 1870s, these had to be licensed by the War Department, but it did little to lower the prices or improve the quality of goods on offer, and most soldiers developed a strong dislike of the sutlers. It was not until 1889 that officially run canteens supplanted the post traders.

Pay day usually resulted in a mass exodus to the nearest post trader or town, if one was close by. Soldiers blew their wages on food, paid off gambling debts, the post laundress and traders, then indulged in a drinking spree that lasted until either the money ran out or the troopers' legs gave out. One man, broke but thirsty, made such a nuisance of himself in the local saloon that in desperation the barkeeper handed him a large full tumbler of whiskey, with the order 'Drink that then get out'. The soldier eyed the glass for a minute, then wordlessly drained it in one go. His friends reported that he woke up 24 hours later apparently none the worse for his excesses.

Those who could afford it would visit the local brothels to indulge in sexual gratification, with the only women accessible to sex-starved troopers. Few were able to form permanent relationships whilst on frontier postings, although occasional marriages did occur between soldiers and female staff at permanent forts – the laundresses or cooks. Some men brought their sweethearts over from the East, but only the strong-willed stayed. For the men who did not avail themselves of the prostitutes, there remained only tantalising glimpses of homesteaders' and officers' wives, and many deserted as a result of this enforced bachelorhood.

Fights were common, and some were serious, resulting in severe disciplinary measures. Other sore-

A classic portrait of Pvt. William E. Riley, US Cavalry, dated around 1886. He wears the 1883 issue slouch hat, 1884 five-button coat and 1884 gauntlets, dark blue flannel shirt, reinforced Cavalry trousers and high boots. His 1885 web belt holds .45-70 carbine ammunition and the holster holds an 1873 Single-Action Colt. (National Archives)

Model 1873 Single-Action Colt in .45 calibre. Probably the most recognisable revolver in the world, the Colt boasts the longest production run of any pistol. This specimen has had its original wood grips replaced by later hard rubber ones. (Board of Trustees, The Royal Armouries)

headed men were fined, given extra fatigues, or if NCOs, they were reduced to the ranks, depending on the degree of insubordination and violence. Some commanding officers, such as Gen. Bradley, regarded the situation as so prejudicial to military discipline, that in 1878 he banned traders from approaching within five miles of his camps in the Black Hills.

Discipline

Few problems were more vexing to commanders than that of maintaining discipline. The problem of desertion has already been touched upon. It was never satisfactorily solved, although the improvements in living conditions, pay and food that came with the reforms of the late 1880s made considerable headway in reducing the number of desertions. The main problem, however, was caused by alcohol rather than the desire to abscond from the rigours of service life. Fights, abusive behaviour and insubordination were the inevitable results of over-indulgence, and the reaction of the Regular Army to such behaviour was often unnecessarily brutal. Justice was usually left to the company officers or senior NCOs, unless the case was particularly serious, in which case the commanding officer would pass judgement, or decide on a court martial. The rank and file had little faith in the impartiality of court martials, and when feasible, the accused man would usually vanish beforehand. Where discipline was left to the whim of the commanding officer, penalties could be unreasonably harsh. George Custer was a strict disciplinarian,

bordering on a martinet, and tolerated no slackness in the 7th Cavalry. Punishments meted out included bucking and gagging (being in a crouched position, with the ankles tied, and wrists fastened to a wooden rod that passed behind the knees), and confinement in an earthen guardhouse with no windows, and a roof too low to permit vertical movement. He illegally instructed one search party to shoot any deserters found. Two were indeed brought back slung over their saddles, the good colonel being subsequently severely censured for the order.

Other officers had a more humane approach, and did not condone unwarranted brutality by any soldier, regardless of rank, although in practice such acts were hard to detect. Fines or hard labour were the most common punishments levied. The loss of a month's wages was a serious blow to a trooper, curtailing his social life to virtually nothing, and such fines would be handed out for the most common of crimes – drunkenness, insubordination, neglection of duty or disobedience. Up to 1874 serious crimes such as murder, robbery and desertion would result in soldiers being confined to state penitentiaries under civilian jurisdiction. After 1874 the US Military prison at Fort Leavenworth was opened, where all military personnel were sent to serve their sentences.

Justice in the frontier army was often an arbitrary affair, and many soldiers of otherwise good character deserted after receiving unwarranted punishments for minor offences. It was only in 1891 that an order was prescribed limiting the punishments that a court martial could hand out. However, soldiers were no angels, and some idea of the level of offences can be gauged from a note appended in the Report of the Secretary of War, stating that 45 per cent of the command of the Department of the Missouri had been tried by the courts in that year!

Food

The rations supplied for the Army campaigning against the Indians were a typical example of Government under-funding. Ration food had never been spectacular in quality or quantity, but during the Civil War, most soldiers had been able to supplement their diet with meat, fruit and vegetables stolen along the way or purchased from post traders and local townspeople, who were only too happy to supply such a lucrative market. Parcels from home were a welcome addition, and most volunteer regiments had company funds upon which to draw to provide extra food when needed. For the most part, such luxuries were denied the troopers stationed in far-flung outposts. Standard rations comprised salt pork, range beef, coffee and hard tack (a solid biscuit, about 4 ins. × 4 ins., which could crack teeth if not softened first with water).

It is certainly true that transportation difficulties made supplying the posts a logistical nightmare. Food, ammunition and clothes had to be hauled by wagon from the nearest rail-heads, usually across miles of hostile country. The teamsters who rode the wagons were tough, brave and determined to profit from their labours. Apart from rations, they brought in barrels of potatoes, apples, onions, butter and eggs. In 1867, at Fort C.F. Smith, it would cost a trooper $2 a pound for butter and $15 (a little over a month's wages) for a bushel of potatoes. Fresh vegetables and dairy produce were not supplied by the Government, and it was not until the late 1880s that canned vegetables were supplied. Occasionally a dried potato or vegetable cake was issued, which when added to water produced a weak soup, but it was not popular. Initially no field cooks were appointed, so men usually took turns at preparing food which was often a recipe for gastronomic disaster! Food was usually boiled, or fried if fat was available, and the skillet was employed for each and every occasion. A system of appointing company cooks was gradually adopted, which was an improvement greatly appreciated by the enlisted men.

Soldiers would forage for anything available, and settlers' pigs, goats and chickens were fair game. Vegetable gardens were popular and encouraged at posts, and these made a valuable nutritional supplement to the diet of the men. Diet-related diseases such as scurvy would occur in poorly supplied outposts, despite the best efforts of officers and men to vary their diet. (During the Sioux Campaign of 1876, Col. Gibbons' column suffered badly from scurvy.) Much of the issue food was left over from the Civil War. In 1866, Pvt. W. Murphy wrote, 'I believe the bacon would have killed the men if it had not been thoroughly boiled ... [it was] yellow with age and

Fort Davis, Texas, circa 1885. Barely comparable with the early forts, Davis was the home to several Cavalry regiments, whose troopers gave sterling service against the Southwestern tribes. (Fort Davis National Historical Site)

bitter as quinine.' Flour was no better, often delivered short measured in sacks with weights in them to make up the loss. One trooper commented, 'The flour had been hauled 65 miles and handled several times. The result was that the refuse left by the mice was well mixed with the flour and we found a number of dead mice in it also. One reason why our rations were so scanty was that the flour was worth $100 a sack.'

Coffee, the staple drink of all US soldiers, was issued green. Beans were roasted over a fire and pounded into granules, usually with the butt of a pistol. Hardtack was useful when it was correctly cooked. Crushed and mixed with fat and bacon, it could be fried, or turned into a form of pudding if boiled in water with stewed prunes or apples.

Not surprisingly, even in the 1880s war-manufactured food was still being issued. Eighth Cavalryman Williamson wrote that 'some of the hardtack . . . was packed in 1863 . . . the hardtack had a green mould on it, but we just wiped it off and they were all right. Most anything tasted good.' Sometimes a remote dwelling would furnish luxuries, such as the small store in Dakota whose proprietress sold cakes and pies. So popular were they that sweet-toothed cavalrymen borrowed from their comrades at $2 for $1 just to sample a pie.

An important addition to the diet was wild game shot by hunting parties – deer, buffalo, wild turkey, jackrabbits, racoon and even prairie dogs were all welcome additions to the pot for a hungry soldier. David Spotts said that when rations had run out, some men tried mule meat, but it tasted foul. After

A typical interior of a barracks in the late 1880s. This was Fort Robinson, but could well have been any fort of the period. Foot lockers, wardrobes, a stove, pool table and weapons rack promise organisation and comforts only dreamed of two decades earlier. (National Archives)

two weeks 'on air and water', he came upon the bivouac of fellow 19th Volunteer Cavalry troopers: 'Gus [gave me] a cigar ... I put it in my mouth and chewed it. I told them ... I would like something to eat. They soon had plenty before me, but I could only eat a cracker and drink a cup of coffee, and that was enough to make me sick for a while'.

COMBAT AND TACTICS

Active service was usually a relief from the monotony of post life. As one Indian campaigner wrote, 'The only real romance in the West is chasing Indians, but fighting them is another story'. Indeed, of the thousands of miles marched by US troops in the West, few actually resulted in contact with the wily enemy. This was partly due to the methods of warfare adopted by the two sides. Army tactics, dating from the 18th century, called for set-piece battles by massed opposing forces. Having established their positions, the two sides would blaze away at each other until one vacated the field. The tactics of the Civil War were hardly different from Crècy, the Hundred Years War or the epic Napoleonic battles. True, the use of firearms had increased distances, and the Cavalry were used less as a battering ram, and more to skirmish, scout and harass supply lines, but the essential method of fighting was the same. To the Indian, this was a total anathema. Indian culture, particularly that of the Plains Indians, placed a very high regard upon personal bravery, and Indians almost never acted as a coherent, commanded fighting unit. When they did, as the Nez Percé and Modocs illustrated, they could prove to be formidable adversaries.

The end result of most campaigns in which cavalrymen found themselves involved was hunger, exhaustion, worn-out horses and equipment, and not more than a fleeting glimpse of Indian scouts keeping a wary eye on the troopers. Private D. Spotts of the 19th Kansas Volunteer Cavalry trekked from Topeka, near Kansas City, south to Fort Sill in Oklahoma, then north to Camp Supply on the Oklahoma/Texas border and up to Fort Hays in West Kansas, between October 1868 and April 1869,

without actually engaging any hostile Indians. Most military contact resulted from lightning attacks on parties of reinforcements, supply wagons and, in particular, fatigue parties, as one wood-cutting party found out in September 1866 at Piney Island, near Fort Phil Kearney. A dozen troopers were working on the timberline when 100 Indians appeared without warning and tried to cut off the party, who sprinted towards a log blockhouse built for such an eventuality. All made it save a Pvt. Smith, who was riddled with arrows and scalped, but astonishingly managed to crawl half a mile to the blockhouse, after snapping off the arrows in his body, to stop them snagging on the undergrowth. His fate is not recorded.

Indian motives for attack were complex. Sometimes they would ignore farmers they regarded as friendly, and massacre the inhabitants of the next dwelling. In other instances, they would murder randomly and seemingly without provocation. In the West, the reason was usually revenge for the unwarranted attacks by settlers and miners who occupied the land, quite often in open contravention of Government Treaties, and treated the native Indians as vermin. In other cases, young braves would launch attacks simply through boredom or a need to prove their manhood.

In the South-west, Kiowa, Navaho, Apache and Comanche raids were less as a result of infiltration by whites, than an intense and consuming hatred of Mexicans. In fact, the Apache chiefs, Mangas Colorados and Cochise, had not been hostile to Americans until 1861 when a misunderstanding over Apache raids led to a series of revenge killings that threw the South-west into turmoil.

Attempting to catch raiding bands was, as one soldier put it, 'Like trying to catch the wind'. In the west, Sioux and Cheyenne would melt into the vastness of the plains, using their intimate knowledge of the ravines, mountains and rivers. Apache and other Mexican border tribes headed for the gaunt and forbidding protection of the Chisos or Chiricahua mountains, or the arid deserts. Even using Indian scouts, the Cavalry often found that instead of being the hunters, they were the hunted. 'The entire detachment was in this dry bed urging the teams through the sand, when to our complete astonishment, a volley of arrows and rifle shots were poured into us. The shots were accompanied with a chorus of savage yells and the timberland and brush above and about us was fairly alive with Indians,' wrote an exasperated Mrs Carrington, an officer's wife.

Many officers who served in the West had the dual disadvantages of a Civil War military education, which was sadly lacking in practical application where Indians were concerned, and a deep-rooted attitude of racial superiority. One of the finest examples in this tradition was Capt. Fetterman, an over-confident Civil War veteran, who had often boasted that given 80 men, he could defeat the whole Sioux nation. He fell for the simplest and most often tried of all Indian tricks, the decoy. On a freezing day on 21 December 1866, ironically along with exactly 80 men of the 2nd Cavalry, he chased a small band of warriors into an ambush of over 2,000 armed warriors. There were no survivors.

How soldiers reacted in combat varied widely. Companies with seasoned veterans in them drew strength from their coolness under fire. During Crooks' pursuit of the Sioux in 1876, a 5th Cavalry rearguard was surprised when the ridge around them suddenly became alive with warriors. Some of the men began to panic and fire into the air, but as Capt. Charles King observed, they were calmed by 'a stalwart bearded fellow commanding the right skirmishers of the company . . . never bending himself, he moves from point to point cautioning such new hands as are excitedly throwing away their shots. He is their first sergeant, a crack soldier'.

Indian attitudes to warfare

It is important to understand the psychology of the men faced with meeting the Indian in combat, for the normal rules of European warfare did not apply. Indians regarded the life of a captured enemy as forfeit, and humane treatment of military prisoners was rare unless they were held for hostage purposes. Indian warriors gained much status from their ability to withstand pain, and trained themselves from youth to bear wounds and injury without complaint. A captive who was tortured to death was held in high esteem if he failed to show pain. Soldiers, however, found this as abhorrent as the Indian practice of

mutilating the dead, which was done to prevent the spirit entering heaven, rather than as a means of desecration. All soldiers dreaded capture, and experienced Indian fighters always had one piece of advice for new recruits, 'Never let them catch you alive – keep the last bullet for yourself'. There is evidence that this was heeded in several instances. During the Fetterman fight, the two surviving officers, their ammunition almost exhausted, placed their revolvers against each other's temples and pulled the triggers. Similar sights were witnessed during the Little Big Horn battle, several warriors later reporting that some troopers had gone crazy and shot themselves. Amos Bad Heart Bull, an Oglala Sioux, who fought at the battle, recounted how a mounted Cavalry sergeant, drawing away from braves who were chasing him, suddenly placed his revolver to his head and killed himself. Pvt. Peter Thompson of the 7th Cavalry, one of Reno's men who survived the subsequent siege, stated categorically, 'I made up my mind that all but one shot would be fired at the Indians and that one would go into my own head for I had determined never to be taken alive.'

Such desperate and decisive actions as fought by Fetterman and Custer were the exception. Generally, engagements were swift and inconsequential, resulting in a few casualties on each side. When surprised by a group of Modocs in May 1873, 5th Cavalrymen

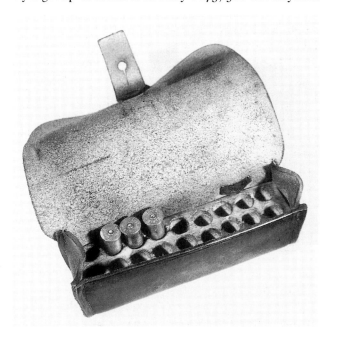

Infantry cartridge pouch modified to hold .50-70 cartridges for use in converted Sharps carbines. (Author's collection)

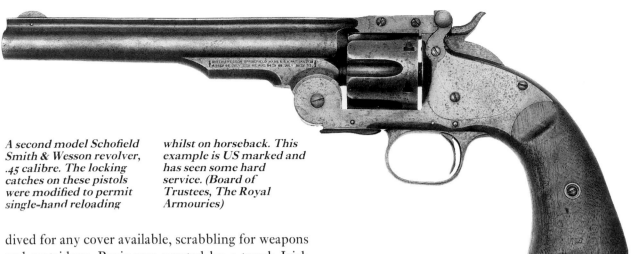

A second model Schofield Smith & Wesson revolver, .45 calibre. The locking catches on these pistols were modified to permit single-hand reloading whilst on horseback. This example is US marked and has seen some hard service. (Board of Trustees, The Royal Armouries)

dived for any cover available, scrabbling for weapons and cartridges. Panic was averted by a tough Irish sergeant, Kelly, who leaped up and yelled, 'God damn it, let's charge ...' The troopers killed five Modocs without suffering any casualties. Set-piece battles between massed opposing forces were very rare, one exception being the battle of the Rosebud on 17 June 1876, when the 1,000-strong column of Gen. Crook met with a similar number of Sioux and Cheyenne. The battle raged for six hours until the Indians withdrew. Crook claimed a victory, but his soldiers had been badly mauled and were forced to return to their supply base.

Most fighting was not done on equal terms, invariably one side outnumbered the others and many 'battles' claimed as victories for the Army were not battles at all, but bloody, one-sided attacks on Indian camps. One example was the Sand Creek massacre of 1868, when 700 volunteer cavalrymen, under a maniacal colonel called Chivington, attacked the peaceful Cheyenne camp of Chief Black Kettle killing 123 men, women and children. George Custer achieved a similar result in the battle of the Washita, when his men attacked another Cheyenne camp. As Capt. A. Barnitz wrote, the cavalrymen came 'crashing through the frozen snow as the troops deployed into line at a gallop and the Indian village rang with unearthly war whoops, the quick discharge of firearms ... the cries of infants and the wailing of women'. In this instance, they met stiff resistance and suffered 19 killed and 14 wounded. Black Kettle and his wife, who had escaped from Sand Creek, were shot down by the cavalrymen.

For the soldiers, such flashes of excitement rarely enlivened their endless trekking across prairie and desert. The men were not politicians or tacticians, and few held any personal animosity against the Indians, often believing them to be victims of circumstance rather than inherently evil. There is no doubt that they feared them, and exposure to Indian methods of killing and mutilation hardened attitudes, but the reaction of troopers to the Indian also depended to a great extent on where they served and their experiences. After Little Big Horn, the 7th Cavalry became renowned as a regiment that hated Indians, finally wreaking their revenge at Wounded Knee in 1890. Units who fought the Nez Percé and Utes invariably held their fighting qualities in high regard, and were more inclined to treat captives kindly. The 6th Cavalry, who had fought a long campaign against the Apache in 1885 in some of the most rugged and inhospitable terrain anywhere on earth, were impressed at the Indians' ability to live and fight in such a land, and upon the surrender of the Apache leader, Nana, expressed open astonishment that the wizened old man could have outwitted the Army for so long.

Much of what the soldiers believed about Indians had come from the mawkish, sentimental and racially biased literature of the period. Mostly they were portrayed as blood-thirsty savages with no morals and little intelligence, except an animal cunning. Many soldiers were intelligent enough to query this view, though some believed that Sherman's dictum, 'the only good Indian is a dead one', was a reasonable viewpoint, particularly if they had witnessed the aftermath of Indian attacks. Long service during the

Indian wars tended to modify ingrained prejudices, and it was clear to many soldiers that white greed and ignorance was the cause of much trouble. Few trusted the Indian Bureau, who kept the reservation Indians supplied, and whose crooked agents often short-changed them, issuing sub-standard food and clothing in place of the issue rations, which they subsequently sold. Sgt. George Neihaus, having fought the Apache, summed up the attitude of many troopers, 'The Indians were promised lots of things, and they were betrayed: then the Indians went out to raid the settlers. I feel the Indian agents, many times – not all – were the cause of a great deal of unrest.'

WOUNDS AND SICKNESS

The rigours of campaign life and the isolation of frontier posts when combined with the limitations of medical science conspired against a soldier unlucky enough to become ill or wounded. Common ailments and diseases were survivable with luck and a convenient hospital. TB and venereal diseases were the most usual afflictions, but cholera and dysentery could decimate a garrison, as Albert Barnitz mentioned in a letter to his wife on 20 July 1867, 'Only think, seven dead men in an evening (all of the 7th Cavalry) isn't a small beginning at all . . . and more the following day. I would much rather see two Indians than one man with the cholera and I am not remarkably fond of Indians either!'

Hygiene was basic and, although the men were expected to bathe weekly, this was often impossible in garrisons where every barrel of water had to be brought in by wagon. Poor sanitation and a tendency to drink any water available when on patrol led to frequent stomach ailments. Most serious cases would be admitted to the post hospital, where if they had a strong constitution and a lot of luck, they might survive to be placed on light duty until eventually recovered.

For those wounded in fights with the Indians, the chances of survival were equally capricious. Bullets of the period were an unpleasant combination of large calibre and soft lead, so a wound anywhere other than a soft, fleshy part of the body was likely to prove serious, with shattered bones and infection being the result. Amputation was the usual treatment for arms and legs, although occasionally skilful nursing would save the limb, albeit leaving the owner with limited use. Indian arrowheads were long and made of thin, soft sheet steel, which deformed badly upon striking a bone. The usual method of removal was to slide a loop of wire along the shaft into the wound, hook the

Soldiers at Fort Keogh in winter 1886. They wear buffalo coats and seal or muskrat hats and gloves. The man on the extreme left has a webbing cartridge belt over his coat. (Little Bighorn Battlefield National Monument)

arrow tip onto the loop, and withdraw both. Peritonitis and gangrene would frequently set in, although a clean wound could heal remarkably quickly. Lance thrusts were invariably deep and fatal, but men could survive apparently fatal gunshot wounds as Albert Barnitz proved. Shot at point blank range by an Indian with a .56 or .70 calibre musket, the ball '. . . struck the lower edge of a rib, and then glancing downward, as I was leaning forward at the time, cut the next rib in two and a piece out of the next rib below where it reflected, and passed through my body and out through the muscle near the spine, passing again through my overcoat and cape'. Despite travelling 100 miles in an ambulance wagon, he recovered and eventually returned to duty. Indians habitually scalped their enemies, involving a circular incision from 2 to 10 ins. across, with the hair and flesh being unceremoniously yanked off. It was also possible to survive scalping, depending on the size of the scalp lifted, although constant headaches and an aversion to extremes of temperature were the usual result.

Statistically, there was more chance of becoming a casualty through illness than as a result of action, with eight men per 1,000 dying from disease, and five per 1,000 as a consequence of wounds, injuries or accidents. One of the most common accidents for cavalrymen was being thrown from their mounts. Trooper Ami Mulford, who wrote a classic account of life as a frontier cavalryman, was crushed by his horse, and discharged crippled at the age of 23. Another was accidental shooting, with most memoirs

covering service during the Indian Wars mentioning at least one death as a result of carelessness or fear.

The quality of Army doctors was questionable too, as the low pay was not likely to attract the more successful and competent. Medical orderlies were untrained, and often men of low ability whose inadequacies did not leave them fit for fighting service. After 1870, Congress exacerbated matters by reducing the number of medical officers from a barely adequate 222 to 192. Presumably none of the Congressmen had ever been forced to wait for a doctor to remove a deeply embedded arrow.

CAMPAIGNS

To understand the difficulties faced by the Army in Indian campaigning, four individual actions are used to illustrate how adaptable commanders had to be to fight and expect any chance of success. In no single instance can any of these actions be taken to be a military success as the modern military historian would understand it. All were gains or losses of a very limited nature, but they show how the Army responded over the period 1865–1890 to the challenge of guerilla warfare. Some commanders, such as Custer, continued with Civil War tactics, and never truly succeeded in fighting Indians on their own terms. Others, like Gen. Miles and Gen. Crook, learned to adapt their tactics to find and fight an elusive and cunning foe.

The Washita, 1868

The battle of Washita on 27 November 1868 is a fine example of traditional mounted tactics, which if used against any European foe, would doubtless have proved a resounding victory for the Cavalry. Throughout the summer, Gen. Phil Sheridan had developed a plan to strike at Indian camps when winter curtailed the warrior's ability to travel and fight. He sent two 'outrider' columns, comprising 3rd Cavalry and 37th Infantry under Maj. Gen. G.W. Getty, 5th Cavalry and 10th Cavalry under Maj. Carr

Another view of soldiers from Fort Keogh. Surviving mid-western winters without such protection led to frequent amputations; temperatures of −60° were not unknown. (Montana Historical Society)

1: Corporal, 1st US Cavalry, 1865
2: Enlisted man's boot, 1872 pattern
3: Enlisted man's Jefferson shoe
4: Civil War pattern holster

A

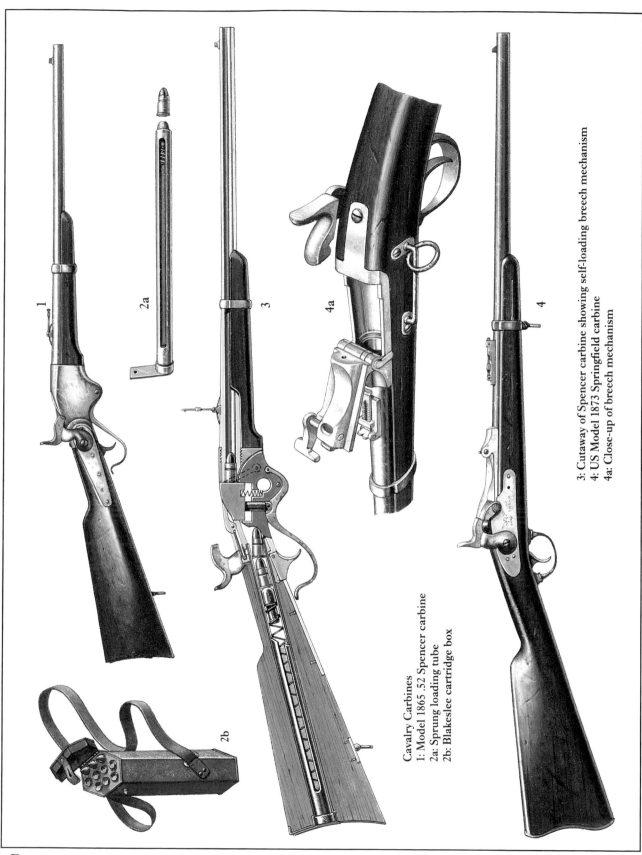

Cavalry Carbines
1: Model 1865 .52 Spencer carbine
2a: Sprung loading tube
2b: Blakeslee cartridge box

3: Cutaway of Spencer carbine showing self-loading breech mechanism
4: US Model 1873 Springfield carbine
4a: Close-up of breech mechanism

B

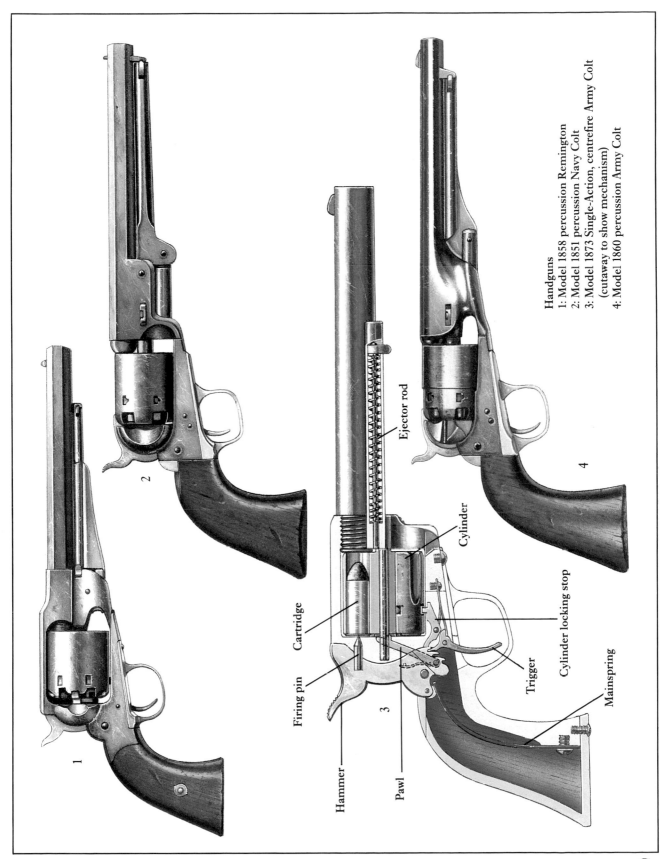

Firing pin

Hammer

Pawl

Cartridge

Ejector rod

Cylinder

Cylinder locking stop

Trigger

Mainspring

Handguns
1: Model 1858 percussion Remington
2: Model 1851 percussion Navy Colt
3: Model 1873 Single-Action, centrefire Army Colt
   (cutaway to show mechanism)
4: Model 1860 percussion Army Colt

1

2

3

4

C

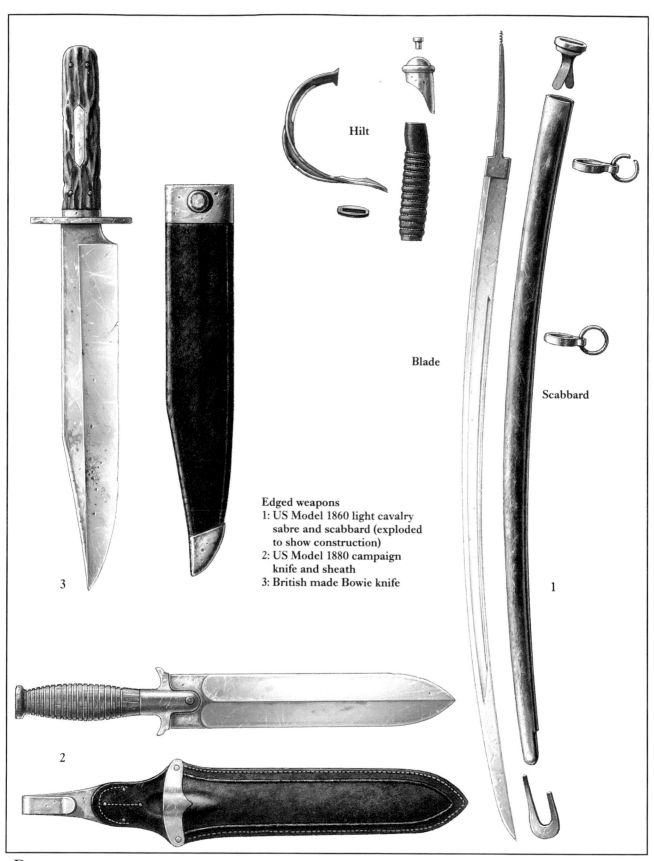

Hilt

Blade

Scabbard

Edged weapons
1: US Model 1860 light cavalry
sabre and scabbard (exploded
to show construction)
2: US Model 1880 campaign
knife and sheath
3: British made Bowie knife

3

2

1

D

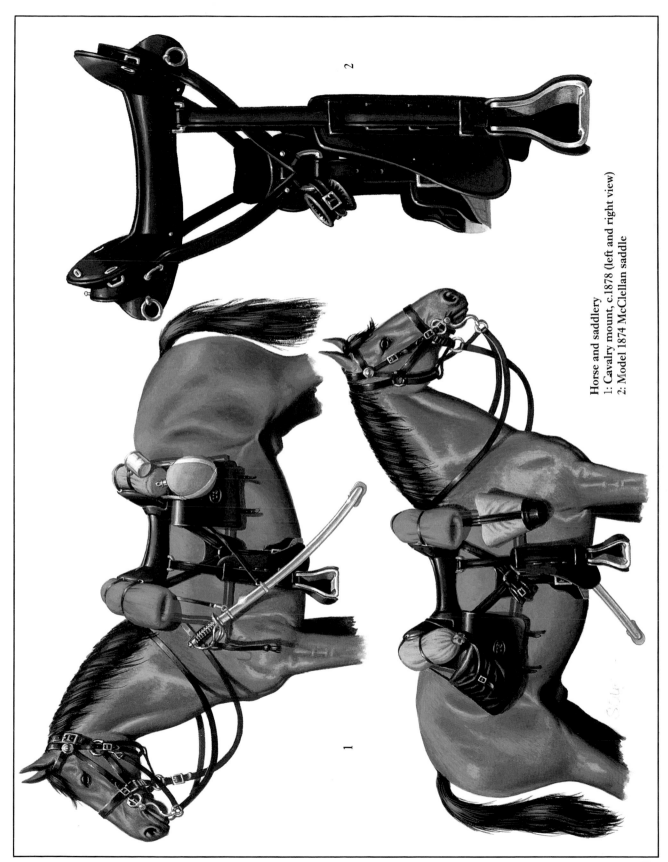

Horse and saddlery
1: Cavalry mount, c.1878 (left and right view)
2: Model 1874 McClellan saddle

E

1: Sergeant, US Cavalry, 1876
2: 1872 forage cap (exploded views)
3: 1855 Hardee hat
4: 1875 campaign hat

F

Cleaning and repair

G

Crook on campaign against the Apaches, Arizona, c.1873

H

Sabre practice, 1874

I

Mounted action, c.1874

J

Dismounted action, c.1885

K

1: Corporal, US Cavalry, cold weather clothing, 1880
2: Buffalo skin coat
3: Buffalo skin hat (exploded to show construction)
4: 1873 canvas and buffalo skin overshoe

L

to drive the hostiles towards his own and Lt.Gen. Sully's column of 11 troops of 7th Cavalry, the 19th Kansas Volunteer Cavalry plus five companies of Infantry, the whole column comprising 800 men.

The pursuit had started badly, as the cold weather deteriorated into heavy, wet snow which lay a foot deep. Hampered by the weather and labouring supply wagons, plus much internal wrangling over command, Sheridan ordered Custer and the 7th Cavalry ahead of the column to try to pick up the hostile trail. After four hard days, during which the horses' grain issue was reduced from 12 to 3 lbs per day, the 7th came upon the Cheyenne camp nestled in a curve of the Washita River. Without ascertaining enemy strengths, or the possible location of other camps, Custer formed his men into four companies and charged. Initially, the attack appeared to have succeeded. Those Indians not killed abandoned the camp and disappeared into the surrounding woods. As the day progressed, the troopers found themselves under increasingly heavy fire from well concealed warriors, who had joined in the defence from a number of campsites spread along the valley, of which Custer had no knowledge. One Cavalry commander, Maj. J.H. Elliott, and 18 cavalrymen were cut off and killed, and Custer was forced to abandon the battlefield, with 21 dead and 14 wounded. The estimate of Indian dead is between ten and 20 warriors and 20 to 40 women and children. The loss of Elliott was to remain a blot on Custer's record for the rest of his service.

The real benefit of the Washita action was not to prove the value of Civil War battle tactics (used against Indians, they were something between wasteful and suicidal), but to prove the soundness of winter warfare. With their accompanying supply train, the cavalry and infantry could wage war at a time of year when Indians traditionally turned to more peaceful occupations. Loss of their campsites meant loss of shelter, foodstocks and horses, forcing them to make a choice – trek to a neighbouring campsite, if one existed, surrender and subsequent transportation to a reservation, or death from exposure or hunger.

Lava Beds, 1872–3

Of all the major actions fought by the Army in the West, this campaign against the Modocs led by Kintpuash proved what determined Indian resistance could accomplish, and gave the Army a chance to commit every military blunder in the book by underestimating the tenacity of their enemy, and overestimating the fighting ability of their own troops. For good measure, the terrain, which is probably unequalled in the United States for barren inhospitality, did not appear to figure largely in the minds of the commanders responsible for waging war on the Modocs.

Trouble had been brewing along the California–Oregon boundary since Kintpuash (also known as Captain Jack) had reluctantly signed a treaty with the US in 1864. The Modocs, Klamaths and Snakes had been moved to reservations, from which a year later the Modocs had moved back to their homelands. In 1872, Gen. Canby was instructed to forcibly return the Modocs – numbering no more than 70 men and their families – to the reservation. An attempt to do so by 40 regulars of the 1st Cavalry was met with a fusillade of gunfire. The result was one dead and one wounded Modoc, two dead and six wounded soldiers and the Indians vanished into lava beds known as the 'Stronghold'. This area comprised acres of jagged waves of frozen rock, full of caves, fissures and interconnecting labyrinths, and the Army was powerless to evict them. Reinforcements of 1st Cavalry and a detachment of 21st Infantry were brought in, as well as two 12 pdr. artillery guns. On the night of 16 January 1873, two attack columns under Maj. Green in the west and Capt. R.F. Bernard in the east edged towards the Stronghold, shrouded in fog. The artillerymen could see no targets and fired blindly, but splinters and rock fragments caused casualties to the troopers, so shelling was stopped. As the soldiers advanced, the silence was shattered by close, accurate fire from hidden Modocs, who probably understood the practical use of a rifle more than any other tribe, and could outshoot the average soldier. For the attacking soldiers, the world suddenly became a nightmare, as recalled in a letter by Lt. H.D. Moore: 'At first fire, the troops were so demoralised that officers could do nothing with them. Capt. Wright ordered his men to take possession of a bluff which would effectively secure their retreat but Capt. Wright was severely wounded ... and his company with one or two exceptions deserted him ... then the slaughter began.' Soldiers who remained at their posts fired

George Armstrong Custer in campaign dress for the Washita, 1869. With the exception of the rather fine buckskin jacket, he would have looked little different from his dusty and bearded troopers. (Little Bighorn Battlefield National Monument)

the Indians that caused their subsequent surrender when a breakaway group under a Shaman called Curley Headed Doctor led cavalrymen to the rebel camp. Kintpuash and three others were subsequently hanged for the murder of Canby at Fort Klamath.

Several lessons were learnt as a result of the campaign, the most important being that it required an Indian to catch an Indian. Scouts had always been employed by the Army, but valuable lives could be saved if renegade tribesmen were co-opted to fight. Once again the Army commanders totally underestimated the ability of their foe, and their attempts to take the Stronghold by direct assault were as foolhardy and wasteful as Polish Lancers attacking German tanks in 1940. Detailed reconnaissance, intimate knowledge of the terrain and adequate numbers of troops were all prerequisites for this form of campaigning which taught Gen. Sherman a costly lesson.

Big Dry Wash, 1882

The campaign in Arizona that culminated in the battle at Big Dry Wash was one of the longest running in the West. It is unusual on two accounts; it was one of the only times that the Army defeated the Apaches, and a rare instance of the Indians engaging in a nearly conventional battle.

Trouble with Apache bands, mainly White Mountain and Chiricahuas, had plagued the Mexican borders for years, but flared into violence over the killing of a Shaman named Nakaidoklini on 30 August 1881. Apache scouts mutinied, killing one officer and six men. Reinforcements of Cavalry served only to create an atmosphere of distrust among the reservation Chiricahua Indians, many of whom fled to join the White Mountain warriors. By the end of the year, Indian depredations had turned the Arizona–New Mexico area into a war zone, killing settlers and policemen, raiding farms and leaving upwards of 200 whites dead. These war parties were led by the most cunning guerilla leaders in history – Geronimo, Chato, Nachez, Juh and Chihuahua – and despite constant exhausting patrols, the cavalrymen had never glimpsed a sight of the hostiles. Some idea of conditions can be gained from the comments made by Surgeon L. Wood, attached to the 4th Cavalry, pursuing Apaches. Their horses had expired in the first week, they were reduced to 'marching every day

blindly, and none even saw an Indian during the entire engagement. The Army lost 11 dead and 26 wounded. The Stronghold was then ringed with bivouacs and observation posts, limiting Indian mobility and access to food and water. Subsequent peace talks failed when Kintpuash shot and killed Gen. Canby and two other peace commissioners. A second assault was launched, the unhappy cavalrymen again being forced to fight on foot. For three days between 15–17 April, two columns slowly advanced through the Stronghold and the Modocs would open fire and then melt away in organised retreat. An advance force under Capt. E. Thomas, of five officers and 59 men, were ambushed in a well-organised attack that claimed the lives of all the officers, 20 men and left 16 wounded. By the time the Army took the Stronghold, there were no Modocs in residence. Ironically, it was internal dissent amongst

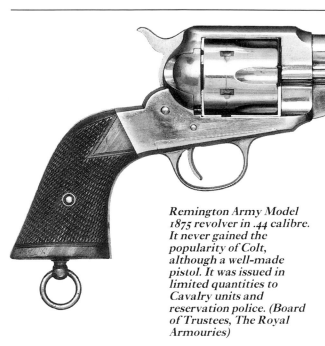

Remington Army Model 1875 revolver in .44 calibre. It never gained the popularity of Colt, although a well-made pistol. It was issued in limited quantities to Cavalry units and reservation police. (Board of Trustees, The Royal Armouries)

in that intense heat, the rocks and earth being so torrid that the feet are blistered and rifle barrels and everything metallic being so hot that the hand cannot touch them without getting burnt. . . . The rain when it does come, comes as a tropical tempest, transforming the dry canyons into raging torrents in an instant. We had no tents and little or no baggage of any kind except rations and ammunition. Suits of under-clothing formed our uniform and moccasins covered our feet.'

After an inconclusive engagement at Horseshoe Canyon between the 4th Cavalry and the Apaches on 23 April, another command, comprising 14 troops of 3rd and 6th Cavalry and a number of Apache scouts commanded by Gen. Chaffee spotted a large body of Apaches under Chief Natiotish in an ambush position on the rim of a canyon. The Indians were engaged with fire, whilst four cavalry troops and some scouts encircled the hostiles, striking at both flanks. The battle raged all day, from dawn to 6 pm, the Indians well concealed but unable to retreat, the troopers working their way forward in the heat and dust from rock to rock, drawing Indian fire until sharpshooters could pick them off. Upwards of 25 Indians died, and it was believed by the attacking troops that none escaped unwounded. Good field command and sound tactics and training had paid off in this instance, but the fact that the Apaches were

forced to fight a pitched battle was a material factor in the success of the Army. It was to take another four years to finally subdue the Apache tribes.

Wounded Knee, 1890

The battle at Wounded Knee has been viewed from many angles, and dubbed a 'senseless massacre' by some historians. It should be borne in mind, however, that the Miniconjou Sioux camped on the Cheyenne River were by no means a settled reservation tribe. Many had been inflamed by the promises of the Ghost Dance, of a new world free of pain and hunger and empty of white men. Some of the radicals such as Kicking Bear and Short Bull took this to mean the destruction of the whites, and the Brulés and Oglala tribes became so aggressive and anarchical that the Indian Bureau panicked, demanding immediate reinforcements. Times had changed in the West over the previous decade. Forts now ringed reservation land, and well-supplied troops could be moved around by railroad. It was ironic that it should have been the 7th Cavalry (who had suffered so grievously at the hands of the Sioux in 1876) who were rushed to intercept the fleeing Chief Big Foot, who they mistakenly believed was leading his Miniconjous to meet with the Oglalas and Brulés. On the morning of 29 December 1890, the 350 Indians awoke to find themselves surrounded by 500 cavalry-men, armed with two quick-firing Hotchkiss guns. Neither side expected a fight, but all were tense, as the order was given for the Sioux to be disarmed. Many hid their guns under their clothing, and when a rifle went off accidentally, chaos ensued. Many troopers closest to the Indians took to their heels, leaving their horses to their own devices. Capt. George Wallace's skull was shattered by a point-blank rifle bullet, as both sides fought in hand-to-hand combat, using pistols, knives and rifle butts. Big Foot, ill with pneumonia, rose to watch and was instantly shot down. Some warriors armed with

Troop C, 3rd Cavalry, at Fort Davis, Texas, 1886. A fine photograph showing troopers in regulation uniforms, and still equipped with sabres, a rare sight by this date.

They wear 1883 campaign hats, and 1884 fatigue blouses, and carry Schofield Smith & Wesson revolvers. (Fort Davis National Historical Site)

Winchesters pumped shot after shot into the confused ranks of troopers. Meanwhile, the soldiers and Hotchkiss gunners on the ridge opened fire, adding to the uproar with the sharp crack of exploding shells. Many troopers across the rim of the hollow were struck by their comrades' bullets, and some closest to the Indians were injured by the shells. After an hour, the shooting subsided as the surviving Sioux fled. One hundred and fifty Indians, including 62 women and children, were killed and 50 wounded. Army losses were 25 officers and men, and 37 wounded.

As a battle, like most that occurred during the Indian Wars, Wounded Knee achieved little in purely military terms. The repercussions could have had disastrous consequences for the Army, for there were over 1,000 armed warriors in camps nearby, and violence seemed inevitable. Fortunately for both sides, Gen. Miles was in overall command, and his understanding of Indian psychology prevented what could have been a disastrous situation. By playing on the divided factions within the Sioux camp, he persuaded them to surrender their weapons. He promised food and shelter for the coming winter, whilst increasing the number of troops around the villages, a careful blend of carrot and stick. Incensed but frightened by the events at Wounded Knee, the Sioux gradually realised there was nothing to be gained by resistance, and they began to drift towards the Agency. On 21 January 1891, Miles's army formed up in procession, and to the sound of 'Garry Owen', the 7th Cavalry's marching song, left the valley. On the hills in the bitter wind, wrapped in blankets and buffalo robes, hundreds of Sioux watched silently as their way of life went with them.

SITES OF INTEREST

Big Bend National Park, Southern Texas
On the edge of the Rio Grande, the park was the base for generations of Kiowa, Comanche and Apache raiders. The landscape is brutal, and unchanged since the years of the Indian Wars.

Big Hole Battlefield, Wisdom, Montana
The site of the clash between Col. John Gibbon and the Nez Percé under Chief Joseph in August 1877.

Buffalo Bill Historic Center, Cody, Wyoming
A wonderful collection of weapons, Indian artefacts and ephemera.

Custer Battlefield, Hardin, Montana
The desolate battle site where Custer and 225 men died on 25 June 1876. There is an excellent museum on the site, and a large graveyard where the victims of the Indian Wars from all over the West are buried.

Fort Abraham Lincoln, Mandan, North Dakota
The base for many expeditions into the Black Hills and the fort from where Custer led his men to the Little Big Horn, and the Cavalry pursued Chief Joseph.

Fort Bowie, Bowie, Arizona
In the remote Apache Pass, this fort was the base for the patrols and larger military operations against the Apaches, directed by Gen. Crook and Gen. Miles.

Fort Buford, Buford, North Dakota
From 1866 to 1870, the fort was the centre of the most

This rough band of cavalrymen are in fact all officers of the 5th Cavalry, photographed in the Black Hills at the close of the Sioux Campaign in October 1876. Their non-issue shirts and hats, neckerchiefs and heavy beards were typical of campaign clothing for all ranks. Visible pistols all appear to be Colt Single-Action. (National Archives)

hostile Indian territory in the West. It was here that Sitting Bull and Gall surrendered after the Little Big Horn. Some original buildings survive and there is a museum.

Fort Davis, Fort Davis, Texas
The base for the Black 9th and 10th Cavalry operating against Apache raiders, the fort has been partially restored and has an extensive programme of living history during the summer months.

Fort Sill, Lawton, Oklahoma
An important post of the Indian Wars, particularly during the Red River Wars 1874–5. It is the burial place of such eminent chiefs as Geronimo, Satanta, Satank and Quanah Parker.

Fort Union, Watrons, New Mexico
Built on the Santa Fe trail in 1851, it was a major supply base for 40 years for campaigns against the

door' Springfield as a backward step, since it was only capable of single-shot operation, having to be re-loaded by hand before each subsequent shot. Its .45 calibre centrefire cartridge was more accurate than the old .52 rimfire, with a slightly greater range. It was a very simple and durable weapon, and served the cavalry from 1873 to the 1890s.

B4a: Close-up of the breech mechanism

Many thousands of Civil War Springfields were converted to the Allin breechloading system. This meant cutting the rear of the breech off, and replacing it with a hinged section which was released by means of a thumb latch. When open, a cartridge could be inserted, the breech was snapped shut, and the hammer manually cocked. Once fired, the catch was released, the block raised and a small ejector pushed the fired case to the rear. In practice, black powder fouling, verdigris and dirt often combined to glue the case firmly in the breech, leaving the unhappy trooper to dig the case out with a knife. If this happened in the midst of a battle, the results could be fatal, and it has been the basis of one explanation for the destruction of Custer's command at the Little Big Horn in 1876.

C: Handguns
C1: Model 1858 percussion Remington

A robust .44 calibre pistol that saw much service during the Civil War and Indian Wars. It was a particular favourite of Indian braves, who used captured examples with enthusiasm. Its solid frame made it less susceptible to damage than the Colts, and it was generally well-liked.

C2: Model 1851 percussion Navy Colt

Manufactured in large numbers for over two decades, the .36 Navy was probably the most common percussion revolver in the west. Although reliable enough, it suffered from the same problem as the .44 Army (No. 4) in that the barrel was only held in place by a steel wedge retained in the cylinder axis pin. The small bullet lacked the power of the bigger .44, and had an effective killing range of only about 25 yards.

C3: Model 1873 Single-Action, centrefire Army Colt

Like the other revolvers illustrated here, the Colt was a single-action pistol, requiring manual cocking for each shot. However, it was the first cartridge revolver adopted by the US Army, and proved to be a reliable and practicable weapon. Cartridges were loaded one at a time through a spring-loaded gate on the right of

First Sgt., John Comfort, 4th Cavalry, in 1877. He wears virtually no issue clothing. His 'sailor' shirt, hat and neckerchief are privately purchased, as apparently are his boots.

His belt is an issue leather one with home-made canvas loops attached. Just visible on his left hip is a large knife. (US Signal Corps)

the frame, behind the cylinder. Cocking the hammer lifted the pawl which engaged in small slots at the rear of the cylinder. This forced the cylinder to rotate one-sixth of a revolution, lining up a cartridge with the barrel. The locking stop then engaged in a slot in the cylinder to ensure that alignment remained perfect. The trigger could then be pulled to fire the gun. A drawback was the slowness of ejecting, which had to be done one case at a time, using a spring-loaded rod in the ejector tube. The .45 calibre bullet was a real man-stopper, however, and in steady hands the pistol was accurate up to 50 yards. So popular was the Colt that it remained in constant production until 1940.

C4: Model 1860 percussion Army Colt

A .44 calibre version of the Navy Colt, it was preferred by cavalrymen because of its larger bullet and greater power. Along with the Navy Colt, it suffered from frame weakness, and if used as a club (not uncommon in hand to hand fighting) it could bend so badly as to be unfireable. Most troopers carried at least a pair of percussion pistols and often several spare loaded cylinders, to save time reloading, which involved filling each chamber with powder, then ramming a lead bullet in using a lever underneath the barrel. A percussion cap then had to be fitted to the nipples at the rear of the cylinder – no easy task in the heat of battle or if one had cold hands.

D: Edged Weapons
D1: US Model 1860 light cavalry sabre and scabbard

The steel scabbard is made in one piece, rolled and then brazed closed, with suspension loops and end shoe also brazed into place. A sprung steel collar fits into the neck of the scabbard, and helps to hold the blade in place. The blade is forged in one piece, with the wooden grip, brass guard and pommel all held in place by a rivet. It was of questionable use in the field, being issued unsharpened, but was undoubtedly a status symbol for cavalrymen. Cumbersome and noisy, it was invariably left behind when on campaign.

A Cavalry officer at Fort Wingate, New Mexico, circa 1886. He wears a shortened 1876 sack coat and has Apache style leggings. His 1881 Mills belt has the 'H' shaped cast brass buckle. He also wears a hunting knife. His hat and neckerchief are not issue items. (Museum of New Mexico)

D2: US Model 1880 campaign knife and sheath

A heavy-bladed, well-made knife with turned wooden grip and brass-mounted leather sheath, this was the first campaign knife issued to the Cavalry, who lacked any form of practical knife for day to day use. It was a tool with myriad uses from opening cans to cutting leather to replace broken harness or equipment. It was even pressed into service as a fighting knife, though few troopers were as adept at using it as the Indians.

D3: British-made Bowie knife

A typical Bowie-bladed weapon, with its distinctive, tapering, false-edged blade, it is a design that can be traced back to the Anglo-Saxon 'scramasax' knife. Many thousands of similar knives were exported to the United States during the latter half of the 19th century, and the example illustrated represents one of the slightly better-quality versions available. It has horn grips and nickel fittings, with an inlaid silver escutcheon in the left grip. The blade is Sheffield steel. The sheath is leather with a silver chape and locket. It could be carried from a leather loop hung on a belt, or simply tucked into the waistband, while some troopers preferred to slide it into a boot top. Virtually every man carried a knife of some sort and it is surprising that the Army did not issue one officially until 1880.

E: Horse and saddlery
E1: Cavalry mount c.1870 (left and right views)

The curb bridle, McClellan saddle and saddlebags are all regulation issue for 1874. This mount is carrying the equipment as officially issued – the blanket roll is carried on the front of the saddle, with rolled forage sack strapped to the rear. The upper illustration shows the sabre slung from its straps and a canteen and cup attached to the rear. The lower illustration shows the trooper's haversack hung from the saddlebag, whilst forward of the saddle is the nosebag. In practice, troopers carried additional gear if the campaign was a long one – extra blankets, greatcoat, and meal sacks with extra rations would all be attached, as well as clothing and additional pistols and ammunition. Generally, troopers tried not to overload their horses, and in hot climates, short pursuits could be undertaken with only the saddle, canteen and some forage and rations carried. This reduced both men and animals to a pitiful state when food and water ran out. Cavalry mounts were selectd from stockbreeders for their size (14–16 hands on average) and temperament, although in practice many fell below this ideal. They suffered badly on campaign with anything up to 75 per cent being rendered 'unfit for service'.

E2: Model 1874 McClellan saddle

Originally designed by Captain George McClellan, 1st Cavalry in 1855, the McClellan became the standard pattern saddle used throughout the Indian wars. The pattern illustrated has the carbine socket and skirts in place, and is in black leather, but saddles could also be found in varying shades of brown and, on campaign, the skirts would often be removed. Extra blankets and a poncho would be put underneath to protect the horse's back and a blanket may also be laid on top of the saddle itself to help cushion

An atmospheric photo of a sergeant walking his horse, whilst on campaign in the South-west, circa 1893. He has the 1885 drab campaign hat, 1883 sack coat and 1885 Mills belt. His one-pint tin mug is clearly visible strapped to the saddlebag. (Arizona Historical Society Wister Collection)

the trooper's behind. The rawhide that covered the McClellan was glued and stitched on to the wooden frame of the saddle, but once soaked and sun-dried a few times on campaign, it soon split, quickly rendering the whole saddle useless. Generally, two years of service was the maximum a McClellan could absorb before needing replacement.

F1: Sergeant, US Cavalry, 1876

This is the regulation issue uniform rarely seen on campaign. He wears the floppy-brimmed 1872 campaign hat, and blouse of 1874 pattern, with branch-of-service piping. His trousers are 1872 issue, with two top-opening pockets, (covered by the blouse); they have been reinforced with canvas at the seat. His carbine sling, sabre belt, holster and sabre are all of Civil War pattern, although the cap pouch visible next to the sword hilt is now used for revolver ammunition. Boots and brass spurs are regulation issue. His carbine is an 1873 Springfield.

This uniform was hot in summer and cold in winter, and had a tendency to rapidly fall apart. Few troopers who started a campaign dressed like this would finish it looking the same.

F2: 1872 forage cap

An improved version of the civil war 'bummer', the 1872 pattern was a more shaped fit, utilising less material in the body, and giving it a less floppy appearance. It was inspired by the French 'Kepi', but was not nearly as smart, and caused no end of problems when worn on campaign. It absorbed water, and provided no protection for the nape of the neck in hot weather. The leather peak would sag and unless a very good fit, the jogging motion of riding would cause the crown to bounce up and down. 'An useless rag' was one of the more printable descriptions of it.

F3: 1855 Hardee hat

A stiff, black, felt hat that pre-dated the Civil War, it was not seen in frontier campaigns in its illustrated form, which depicts an officer's pattern with gilded wire insignia. When on campaign, the feather was usually removed, the flapped brim dropped down, and the crown pummelled into a more comfortable shape. All wool-felt hats suffered badly in the rain, and the Hardee, like the trooper's wide-brimmed hat, would have sagged badly when wet. It was not used beyond about 1870, most troopers preferring civilian made items.

Troopers of the 7th Cavalry at Pine Ridge, before Wounded Knee, 1890. For the most part they wear 1884 blouses, with issue leather and canvas looped belts and

1879 leather holsters. At least one man (seated on the wheel) retains his early full-flap holster. (Denver Public Library, Western Historical Dept)

F4: 1875 campaign hat

An attempt by the Army to produce a serviceable hat after the badly designed, wide-brimmed, 1872 slouch hat. It was of wool-felt construction with leather sweat band and was based on the popular East Coast, broad-brimmed slouch hat. It had a small vent-hole each side of the crown, and was a creditable attempt at solving the problem of functional headgear. Soldiers, however, still preferred to purchase civilian hats, and the 1875 never became popular.

G: Cleaning and repairs

NCOs cleaning up after a campaign, c.1879. These men are wearing a practical mixture of regulation and non-regulation clothing, indeed only the yellow rank-stripes on their trousers indicate they are actually soldiers. Campaign life could be very tough on animals and weapons, and cleaning up was always a priority on return from campaign. The horse was every trooper's first concern. Each man was responsible for the maintenance of his mount and equip-

ment, and penalties could be severe if he failed to take good care of them. The man at the left tends to the grooming of his horse, prior to his personal grooming, which will involve a visit to the post's barber for a haircut. Rifles and pistols suffered badly in the Midwest through the effects of rain, grit and sun, and if any action had been seen the black powder residue in the firearms would quickly turn into a corrosive acid. Rudimentary cleaning kits were carried, but time did not always permit proper care to be taken of firearms or swords. Carbines with broken stocks, revolvers with broken main-springs or jammed cylinders could not be repaired in the field, and would be exchanged on return to camp for serviceable weapons. Most major posts had an armourer, blacksmith and harness-maker to repair or refurbish damaged equipment and weapons. What could not be repaired was returned to depot for exchange. Sabres rusted very quickly, and it was nearly impossible to keep them clean in the field. The NCO illustrated here is using an oily rag to burnish the blade. If rust was very bad the post armourer would file it off, and re-polish the blade as best as he could. Old shirts and blankets were highly valued as cleaning rags, as the Army did not provide such necessities. Officers had the luxury of a groom who would take care of their horses, and a personal servant who was responsible for his uniform and equipment.

H: Crook on campaign against the Apaches, Arizona c.1873

Of all the South-western tribes, the Apaches were probably the most cunning, cruel and hardy. Gen. Crook was not a man to underestimate his enemy, and he made full use of the adage, 'It takes an Apache to catch an Apache'. Using trusted native scouts, his cavalry were able to track their enemy into the inhospitable deserts of Texas, New Mexico and Arizona. White Army scouts were also a valuable asset, once they had learned the Apache ways of fighting and how to best survive in the pitiless heat. Many adopted Indian ways of dress, as illustrated here, with high leg moccasin boots, to protect against plants like the Spanish Bayonet, whose razor-edged, spiked leaves could cut to the bone. Ambush was the most common form of attack, and troopers had to be on their guard. Gen. Crook habitually carried a short-barrelled shotgun (deadly at close range) and the Cavalry scout wears his revolver in a civilian-type open-topped holster, making the pistol more accessible in a hurry.

The Apache scout is examining a trail for signs of activity. Good scouts could track horses across rock by detecting signs that would be invisible to a white man. Most native scouts were armed with the latest weapons, and this man has the Springfield rifle as issued to the infantry. Wherever possible, they would equip themselves with captured or purchased firearms, and it was not uncommon for scouts to be armed with more modern weapons than regular troopers.

The harshness of the climate exacted a terrible price from both men and animals, and horses could collapse after a week on patrol. Crook always favoured the mule, more sure-footed than a horse and generally hardier. Apache warriors would use horses until they dropped, then switch to another, often eating the first animal after it expired. Although eventually won over by promises of food and reservation lands, the Apache were never truly subdued, despite being constantly outnumbered. US troopers were impressed at the Apache's ability to survive in a land that conspired against all forms of life.

I: Sabre practice, 1874

Training for recruits was rudimentary at best, and proper facilities for initiating troopers into Cavalry life were not provided until the 1880s. Many post commanders were concerned at this lack of instruction and took it upon themselves to ensure men were given at least basic training. In this illustration, a trooper is practicing sabre drill, a notoriously difficult skill to master.

The sabre was designed for both piercing and slashing, and it required considerable dexterity to control a galloping horse and wield a sword at the same time. In theory, a charging cavalryman should hold the sabre straight out in front of him, with his wrist twisted round to the right. This ensured the curved, sharp edge of the sabre was uppermost with the point angled down, so that when striking an enemy the weight of the blow forced the blade up and out of the body, preventing it becoming stuck, and being dragged from the trooper's grasp as the victim fell. In practice, this rarely happened, as excited soldiers slashed at any brave who came near, usually with little effect. In practical terms, the sabre was of little use in plains warfare, particularly as the Indians made increasingly effective use of firearms. Although they felt great affection for the sabre, few troopers had cause to use it in anger, but it remained in service as a symbol.

J: Mounted action, c.1874

The US Cavalry seldom excelled in open warfare with Indians, being unable to match them in endurance, stealth and cunning. Most 'victories' were against encamped Indian bands as illustrated here. This reconstruction shows well the variety of uniforms and weapons that could be found in a troop. The man in the foreground is using a .45 Colt and carrying a newly-issued 1873 Springfield carbine, whilst the man on the right shoots a .50/70 Sharps – affectionately known as 'Ole Reliable'.

Indians caught by surprise were seldom able to reply with the same volume of firepower; generally they were more concerned with ensuring their women and children were moved to safety. As a result, casualties were often heavy, with few losses to the troopers.

Material losses, particularly in winter, were often more serious to the Indians, as their food, clothing and ponies were captured or destroyed. There was little braves could do in the face of a Cavalry charge, particularly if the Cavalry commander was shrewd

2 pdr. Hotchkiss gun used at Wounded Knee. The soldier kneeling to the left wears a muskrat cap and

webbing belt with the brass 'US' buckle, first adopted in 1872. (Library of Congress)

nowhere was safe, particularly in winter. Wherever they went, the US Cavalry followed.

K: Dismounted action, c.1885

A skirmish in the South-west. The troopers have dismounted to take up defensive positions as laid down in the Army manual. Working in groups of four, one man was detailed to hold the reins of the horses, whilst the other three fought on foot, working forward with the other men of the company in an effort to push the hostiles back. This was a good tactic in theory, but against Indians, theory usually broke down. The Indians rapidly realised that without their mounts, cavalrymen were no match for them, so they attempted to scatter the horses, and the soldier guarding them was the primary target. Many braves carried bone whistles which gave out a piercing shriek often causing the animals to bolt. Such tactics were used very successfully on Maj. Reno's command at the Little Big Horn.

Two of the troopers illustrated have abandoned their jammed Springfield carbines and are using their .45 Colt revolvers, but once these were empty, the soldiers would be virtually defenceless until they

enough to deploy his men in two 'pincer' columns. For the cavalrymen, the thrill of a charge compensated for the frustrating hours of chasing an invisible foe. Accusations of unnecessary brutality were often levelled at the troopers, but in the dust, confusion and excitement, it was difficult to keep a clear head. Sometimes unplanned acts of heroism occurred. On one occasion a trooper's horse bolted during an attack on a Sioux encampment, carrying the terrified man right through the village. On reaching the safety of the other side, the trooper reloaded his revolver with shaking hands, at which point his horse, presumably missing the company of the other troop mounts, promptly bolted back again. The bewildered trooper was subsequently awarded the Medal of Honor for gallentry. Others weren't so fortunate, and any man unhorsed in an attack was doomed, for there was rarely time for a bunky to go back for him. Such attacks whilst glorious, were infrequent and ineffectual, but did serve to show the Indians that could reload. Cavalrymen reduced to fighting on foot were rarely able to defeat Indians, a fact of which both sides were only too aware.

L1: Corporal, US Cavalry, cold weather clothing, 1880

Troopers feared the cold much more than the heat, which they accepted as normal for the West. As with most issued equipment, the clothing supplied was inadequate to cope with the cold. The caped overcoat illustrated was neither wind nor waterproof, and even when worn with a rubber poncho was insufficient for winter temperatures that chilled a cup of coffee as soon as it was poured from the pot. Gauntlets were worn most of the time, to keep the hands warm, and to stop the reins chafing. In very cold conditions, fur overmitts would be worn, and the coat stuffed with straw or dried grass to provide an insulating layer. The rubber and canvas boots were an improvement on the issue boot, but were cumbersome and impractical for riding. Warm headgear was always a problem. Slouch hats stuffed with straw then tied on the head with a wool scarf provided a partial solution, but were hardly ideal. A fur hat, such as the Buffalo skin example shown here, was by far the best solution, when such an item could be obtained.

L2: Buffalo skin coat

Indians particularly relied upon the buffalo for clothing in winter, and US troopers rapidly copied this practice. The coat illustrated has a quilt cotton lining and would most likely be owned by an officer, although many troopers purchased them. Some were brought with company funds and were handed out to men on guard duty, each sentry passing the coat onto the next. Freezing to death on guard was common, and such coats were vital for survival.

L3: Buffalo skin hat

Hats of this pattern were worn throughout the Indian Wars. Some, like the one illustrated, were of buffalo, others were made of seal, muskrat or beaver. The hat could be folded down to provide good protection for the ears and neck, but a good thick scarf would still be needed, as the nose was particularly susceptible to frostbite. It was one of the few items of headgear that was popular with the troopers.

A fatigue party of troopers at Fort Grant, Arizona, circa 1880. The only clue to their military background is the guard on the right. (Arizona Historical Society)

L4: 1873 canvas and buffalo skin overshoe

Although clumsy the overshoes were partly successful as they provided much needed insulation for the feet. Few cavalrymen survived a winter campaign in ordinary boots alone without the loss of a few toes, for the feet were notoriously difficult to protect. Thick felt overboots, stuffed with straw worked quite well if a soldier was on sentry duty; and a later pattern rubber 'Arctic overshoe' went some way towards providing full waterproofing. However, no suitable compromise was ever reached that enabled the trooper to ride and keep his feet warm. As a result cavalrymen adopted a wide range of civilian footwear.

Bibliography

Barnitz, Albert & Jenny. *Life in Custer's Cavalry*, Ed. R.M. Utley (Lincoln, Nebraska 1988)

Betinez, Jason, with W.S. Nye. *I fought with Geronimo* (Harrisburg, Pennsylvania 1959)

Bourke, John G. *An Apache Campaign in the Sierra Madre* (New York 1958)

Brown, Dee. *The Fetterman Massacre* (Lincoln, Nebraska 1972)

Brown, Dee. *Bury My Heart at Wounded Knee* (London 1972)

Carrington, Frances C. *Army Life on the Plains* (New York 1971)

du Mont, John S. *Custer Battleguns* (Canaan, New Hampshire 1988)

Hutchins, James S. *Boots & Saddles at the Little Bighorn* (Ft. Collins, Colorado 1976)

Katcher, Philip. *US Cavalry on the Plains, 1850–90* (London 1985)

Katcher, Philip. *The American Indian Wars, 1860–90* (London 1977)

King, Capt. Charles. *Campaigning with Crook* (Norman, Oklahoma 1989)

Marquis, Thomas B. *Keep the last bullet for yourself* (Algonac, Michigan 1987)

Marshall, S.L.A. *Crimsoned Prairie* (New York 1972)

Mulford, Ami F. *Fighting Indians in the 7th U.S. Cavalry* (New York 1899)

Reedstrom, Ernest L. *Bugles, Banners and War Bonnets* (Caldwell Idaho 1977)

Rickey, Don. *Forty Miles a day on Beans and Hay* (Norman, Oklahoma 1989)

Spotts, David L. *Campaigning with Custer* (Lincoln, Nebraska 1988)

Steffan, Randy. *The Horse Soldiers, Vol II, 1851–1880* (Norman, Oklahoma 1987)

Stewart, Edgar. *Custer's Luck* (Norman, Oklahoma 1987)

Time-Life Books. Ed. Constable, George. *The Soldiers* (New York 1972)

Urwin, Gregory J. *The United States Cavalry* (New York 1985)

Utley, R.M., and Washburn, W.E. *Indian Wars* (New York 1985)

Utley, R.M. *Bluecoats and Redskins* (London 1973)

GLOSSARY

Black Powder A mix of 15 per cent charcoal, 10 per cent sulphur and 75 per cent potassium nitrate. A propellant used for all cartridges up until about 1890.

Bowie A large fighting knife whose invention was incorrectly accredited to Col. J. Bowie. It has a single-edged blade, with curved false edge. Many were very large, measuring a foot in length.

Buckskin A strong soft thick leather made from deer or goatskin. Usually yellow or fawn in colour.

Bummer The Civil War kepi, made of blue wool with a leather peak, it was generally regarded as useless as headwear.

Bunky A bunkmate, or good friend.

Col. Miles (centre), staff and troopers brave a Montana winter prior to attacking the Sioux in 1877. They wear an assortment of privately purchased fur coats. The officer at the left also has matching knee boots. (National Archives)

Calibre The internal dimension of a barrel.

Cantle The raised rear portion of a saddle.

Carbine A rifle of reduced barrel length, usually firing a reduced power cartridge.

Centrefire A cartridge with a primer mounted centrally in its base. Of greater strength than the rimfire. It could be easily reloaded once fired. In general use from about 1872.

Cholera An intestinal disease caused by impure water. Usually fatal.

Colt A company formed by Samuel Colt (1814–1862) who pioneered mass production and parts interchangeability. The revolver design, although not invented by Colt, was effective enough to gain military interest, and from 1847, the factory was engaged in producing a wide range of pistols.

Double-action A firearm that can be fired by squeezing the trigger, without first manually cocking the hammer.

Ejector A spring-loaded rod which enabled fired cases to be removed from the cylinder of a revolver.

Entry and Exit Wounds A self-explanatory term; the exit wound of a bullet is usually two to four times greater in size than the entry wound.

Fatigues Either a general term relating to work undertaken, e.g. cookhouse fatigues, or a specific term applied to the loose white jacket and trousers issued to prevent soiling of the service uniform.

Gate-loading Single-action revolvers (e.g. Colt .45) had fixed cylinders. Cartridges had to be loaded one at a time through an aperture (gate) at the rear.

Garry Owen A popular Irish tune adopted as the marching song of the 7th Cavalry.

Gatling Gun The invention of Dr. R. Gatling (1818–1903). It had six rotating barrels, but was cumbersome and heavy being mounted on an artillery carriage.

Gun Powder see **Black Powder**.

Hash A meal consisting of fried meat, mixed with anything else that was available – crushed biscuit, vegetables or bacon fat.

Hotchkiss A small quick-firing, 2 pdr. cannon which used high explosive or case shot. Often used with great effect in remote areas inaccessible to artillery.

Jerky Dried beef. It looked and tasted like boot leather but was nutritious and often all that was available.

Kepi A peaked cap based on the French military pattern.

Kersey A coarse woollen cloth, not renowned for its longevity.

Lariat A length of rope carried on the saddle.

Lever-action Rifles such as Winchesters, which could be cocked by use of a hand lever forming part of the trigger guard.

Magazine A tube containing cartridges one of which

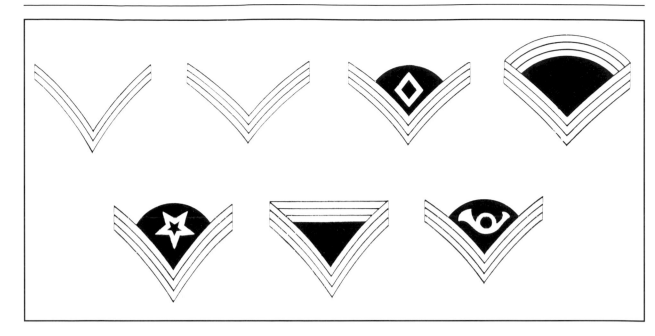

1872-pattern cloth chevrons for cavalry specified in General Order No. 76, dated 27 July 1872. Top, left to right: corporal, sergeant, first sergeant, sergeant major. Bottom, left to right: ordnance sergeant, quartermaster sergeant, principal musician.

would be loaded into the breech upon cocking.

Mills Belt A woven cotton belt of the type normally now referred to as webbing. Reputed to have been invented by Capt. Anson Mills, US Cavalry.

Mutilation A practice favoured by Indians, which involved removal of limbs and organs, or deeply slashing the corpse with knives or tomahawks. It was done to prevent the spirit of the dead ascending to the afterlife. Troopers found the practice abhorrent.

Muzzle The forward end of a barrel.

Percussion A form of ignition relying on the hammer striking a copper cap filled with fulminate.

Pommel The raised 'horn' at the front of a saddle, providing an anchor point for a rope, resting place for a carbine and hand grip in rough terrain.

Poncho A rubberised cape, designed to be worn mounted or on foot. Two could be joined together to form a small tent.

Rawhide Natural, untreated cow leather.

Remington Founded in Ilion, New York, by Eliphalet Remington in 1816, the company made a large number of solidly contructed firearms, including the .44 Army revolver and Rolling Block rifle.

Rimfire A cartridge detonated by the firing pin striking the edge of the case, which contains a fulminate priming compound. Rimfires were structurally weak, and could not be reloaded once fired.

Sabre Specifically a curve-bladed Cavalry weapon, designed for slashing.

Sack Coat The four- or five-button service tunic. So called because of its fit.

Scurvy Vitamin deficiency – it resulted in loss of teeth and hair and bleeding gums. In extreme cases it could be fatal.

Shaman An Indian holy man regarded by many as a prophet. Often held more authority than tribal chiefs.

Sharps A breech-loading percussion rifle patented by Christian Sharps (1811–1874) in 1848. After the Civil War, hundreds of the rifles were produced using centre-fire cartridges and were used in great numbers for buffalo hunting.

Single-action A firearm that requires the hammer to be manually cocked before each shot.

Sling A wide, leather shoulder belt with a snap-hook designed to carry the carbine whilst on horseback.

Smith & Wesson Formed by Horace Smith (1808–1893) and Daniel B. Wesson (1825–1906) the company began making hinged-frame revolvers which evolved into the self-ejecting models of 1869. Arguably better designed than the Colts, the company were a major supplier of pistols.

Snowbird Army slang for a deserter.

Spencer A magazine-fed, rimfire rifle patented by Christopher Spencer (1833–1922) in 1860. It was the first metallic-cartridge, repeating firearm used in warfare.

Stable-frock A white, loose-fitting jacket worn to protect the uniform during fatigues.

Surcingle A wide, woven strap that covers both saddle and girth on a horse for added security.

Sword knot A leather wrist-strap to prevent the trooper dropping the sword if he loosens his grip.

Top-break The system of unlocking a revolver to extract the cartridges. A latch forward of the hammer would be lifted, allowing the hinged barrel and cylinder to drop forward and down.

Verdigris A green mould that always appears on copper or brass that is in contact with leather.

Winchester The company founded by Oliver Winchester (1810–1880) based on the Volcanic Arms Company, who produced an early lever-action repeating pistol. His Henry repeating rifle (1860) was used in limited numbers during the Civil War, and the improved Winchester model became one of the most popular rifles in the West.

The American Plains Indians

Introduction

The central plains of North America, to the east of the Rocky Mountains, provided the homeland for the Plains Indians; here the hunting grounds of the twelve 'typical' tribes coincided with the grazing range of the largest of the buffalo herds. These tribes all shared the common features of extensive use of the tipi, buffalo and horse; the division of warriors into societies; and the religious ceremony called the Sun Dance. Cultural characteristics naturally varied from tribe to tribe, most obviously between the least associated tribes such as the Blackfoot to the north and the southerly Comanche. The Plains tribes inevitably had links with their neighbouring tribes on the borders of the Plains. To the west were the Plateau tribes, such as the Nez Percé; and the south-west desert tribes, such as the Apaches, had originally been among the earliest inhabitants of the Plains. They, like the village farming tribes on the borders of the eastern woodlands, because of their close proximity to the Plains Indians shared with them a number of cultural traits, and in fact occasionally ventured out on to the open grasslands themselves.

The Plains Indians established themselves during a period which is referred to as 'dog-days', because the dog provided their only beast of burden. Most tribes initially ventured west from the eastern woodlands, across the prairies and on to the Plains. However, these pedestrian Indians were unable fully to exploit this hostile environment until after the introduction of the horse, which, by allowing the successful hunting of the buffalo and the adoption of a fully nomadic life, encouraged many tribes to abandon border areas for the central Plains. The adoption of a horse culture heralded the golden age of the Plains Indians—an age abruptly ended by the intervention of the white man, who forced them from their vast homelands into reservations in the second half of the 19th century.

The transitional period of movement on to the open Plains occurred in most cases during the 17th century, although the previously mentioned tribal variations make exact dating impossible. Similarly, while certain characteristics can be considered typical of the Plains Indians as a whole, it is important to note that there were usually variations, both from tribe to tribe and between individuals. Indeed, their society was highly individualistic, partly because they were a very spiritual people. Their life was not centred on physical survival, but on spiritual renewal, and much of it focused on maintaining harmony with the Sacred Powers. The word 'medicine' has come

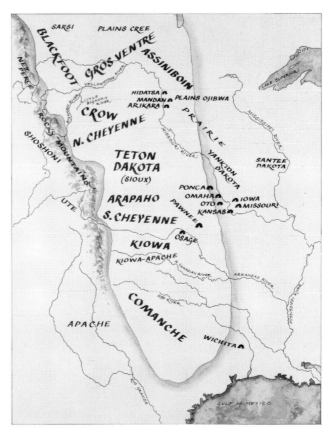

Map showing historic location of the Plains tribes, indicated here in large capitals. Sedentary 'village' tribes are indicated by the earth lodge symbol.

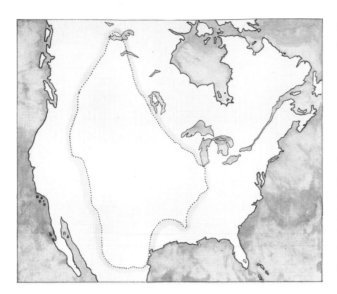

Map showing distribution of the buffalo herds, c.1800—compare with tribal map.

the other side of this tragic but inevitable clash of cultures.)

Community Structure and Camp Life

The divisions of the Plains Indians were far more complex than simply those between tribes. Each tribe was closely related to a number of others linguistically, from the time before movement on to the Plains began. There were also more distinct tribal divisions, and subsequent ramifications into sub-tribes, hunting bands and clans.

The Sioux nation, for example, was initially divided into three separate entities over a period of time: the Dakotas, or Santee Sioux; the Nakotas, or Yankton Sioux; and the Lakotas. While the first two tribes remained on the eastern edge of the Plains, the Lakotas or Teton Sioux migrated west to the central Plains, and became known as the Western Sioux. The Assiniboin tribe were also an off-shoot from the Yankton Sioux, following a later dispute.

Although the number fluctuated slightly as divisions disbanded or united, there were strictly seven sub-tribes of the Teton Sioux, this number being considered integral to the nation's structure. These were the Brulé, Hunkpapa, Miniconjou, Oglala, Oohenonpah, Sans Arcs and Sihasapa.

Even these sub-tribes still contained too many people to be practical units outside the summer months. Just as the summer buffalo herds dispersed into small groups as the grass became less plentiful, so the Plains tribes divided up into compact hunting bands. These were small enough to be mobile and to require only a limited amount of food and grazing, while remaining large enough to defend themselves and to co-operate as a unit, for instance when hunting buffalo. The bands, comprising approximately 20 to 30 families in the case of the Blackfoot, were identified by nicknames. The Oglala Sioux, for example, were divided at one time into six hunting bands or 'tiyopses': the Oglala, Red Water, Old Skin Necklace, Nightcloud, Red Lodge and Short Hair.

The hunting band was the basic working unit for most of the year, until the whole tribe gathered for

to describe the supernatural or spiritual power which the Indians personally received from their deities, and which guided them in hunting, war, healing, and all the other concerns of everyday life.

As a nomadic people their borders were vague, and—in contrast to the men who forced them from it—the Plains Indians had no conception of actually owning the sacred Mother Earth.

Given the special and integrated nature of Indian life and attitudes, it is inevitable that this short study of their culture departs somewhat from the normal Men-at-Arms format. The Plains Indians had no specifically military organisation in the European sense. Their approach to warfare is described in the pages which follow, but only as one aspect of their overall nature. The greater part of Plains Indian history must be seen against a background of constant small-scale warfare between tribes and smaller groups. Their confrontations with the blue-coated soldiers who finally destroyed their independent existence occupied only a few decades, and were not typical of the Indian experience. Those final years demonstrated vividly the enormous gulf which lay between Indian and white attitudes to warfare; and there is a danger of slipping into misleading generalisations if we attempt to analyse the Indian experience through the distorting perspective of the white man's military culture and assumptions. (Another Osprey book entitled *The US Cavalry on the Plains, 1850–90*, written by Philip Katcher, No. 168 in the Men–at–Arms series, describes the summer's hunts and ceremonies. While its size fluctuated to some degree, since members were generally free to move to a more successful band, each unit was comprised mainly of relatives by blood or marriage, a practice which obviously encouraged group unity. This was taken to a greater degree in some tribes by the establishment of clans, whereby affiliation was fixed either patri-locally or matrilocally. The exogamous nature of most bands and clans also served to prevent marriage between relatives, a practice of whose dangers the Indians were keenly aware.

Harmony within the individual hunting bands and in the tribe as a whole was maintained by a number of 'chiefs'. The tribe was considered to be one large family, the camp circle symbolising the family tipi, and the chiefs were at its head. While the structure of each tribe's authorities was complex, the most general distinction between leaders was that between war chief and civil chief. The civil chiefs were generally senior, older men, concerned with the day to day life of the tribe; while war chiefs—the officers of the warrior societies—were vigorously involved in martial affairs. Rôles of authority also extended to groups of respected elders; and to shamans—both in their own right, as for instance when directing the search for buffalo, and as recognised chiefs.

The idea of the Plains Indian chiefs as autocrats is mythical. The many leaders of each tribe held rôles of varying titular superiority, but all enjoyed only limited authority. Even if one band's chief was recognised as the tribe's head man, his rôle would simply be to chair the tribal council. The leaders of the hunting bands would act only in an advisory capacity, so that their authority was only as great as their personal influence. A poor chief would soon lose his position, while the band of a popular leader would prosper and expand. Consequently, to become a chief a man had to display all the virtues expected of a good man. Ideally this meant that anyone could become a chief through leading an exemplary life, although in reality opportunity was sometimes greater for the son of an established leader.

Inspired by the prestige of their elders, young men were certainly keen to follow the path to chieftainship, which lay initially through acquiring the status necessary to lead war parties. A

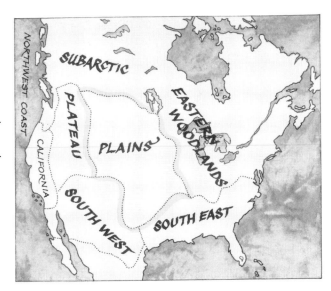

The main cultural divisions of the North American Indians.

recognised warrior could attain advantages in council, both in when he spoke and how much heed was paid to his word. By displaying the other virtues expected of a chief—good sense, honesty, even temper, personal responsibility and unceasing generosity—an aspiring leader set a good example, placed others in his debt, and slowly increased his influence. Since they clearly had to lead by example, the Indians stated that their chiefs were not elected but 'just got that way'.

Important tribal matters were discussed and resolved by the council, one of the most advanced of which was the Council of Forty-Four of the Cheyenne. This comprised 40 chiefs drawn from the ten bands and four Old Man Chiefs, and was guided by a set of regulations (forbidding, for example, the killing of one Cheyenne by another). The council, which met in summer to make decisions for the tribe, represented a strict democracy; working closely with the men's societies, and recognising the wishes of the people, it only made decisions which could be supported by the majority of the tribe.

Since a chief's authority was really only paternal, a good deal of personal responsibility was demanded from each individual. Usually a destructive member of the community was initially reasoned with rather than reprimanded, and there was ample incentive for everyone to make their contribution. Firstly, correct behaviour was in-stilled into youngsters by the example of the proud, honoured chiefs and warriors. Secondly, the survival of the hunting band was dependent on a co-operative effort, and the obligation was increased by the fact that every member was surrounded by so many close kin. Indeed, the necessity for a band to be able to assign tasks and pool resources promoted the idea that it was good to increase your number of relatives. The convention of treating even quite distant members of the extended family as immediate relatives also fostered unity, and generally ensured that no one was left destitute.

The obligation to marry into a different band helped to maintain the various elements of the tribe as a whole. Whether the man or the woman moved to join the band of their in-laws, the bands were drawn together by blood, and the tribal camp in the summer was eagerly awaited as an annual reunion.

An individual's behaviour was also kept in check in more direct ways, particularly by the importance placed upon public opinion. His standing in relation to his fellow tribal members was central to the Indian's philosophy. Accordingly, while great prestige awaited the virtuous man, ostracism was the punishment of selfishness, cowardice, laziness or dishonesty. The Blackfoot apparently subjected deviants to such public mockery and abuse as to sometimes drive them into exile or on to the war-path; while the Crow formalised such punishment by the recognition of 'joking relatives', who as well as bantering with each other were also expected to shame one another out of deviations in conduct. If such warnings as these, or those from a headman, went unheeded, the council were empowered to exile a man, or to sanction a warrior society to punish him, for instance by destroying his lodge and possessions.

The Tipi

The lodge or 'tipi' provided shelter for all the tribes of the Plains; even the more static village tribes such as the Hidatsa, Mandan and Arikara employed them when they travelled away from their earth lodges. It remains one of the best designed tents in the world today, and was admirably suited to life on the Plains.

The tipi was basically a tilted cone, comprising three or four main poles strapped together at the top with sinew, interspersed with lighter, strengthening poles, and covered with dressed buffalo skins. The lower quarter also had a draught-excluding buffalo-hide liner on the inside, and a narrow entrance facing east was covered with a skin flap.

The main asset of the tipi was its mobility. It could be transported easily, the poles presenting the greatest encumbrance; and with the advent of the horse it became practical to expand it to an average 15 ft base diameter, when it required only two or three horses to drag the poles and carry the lodge-cover. The tipi could be dismantled or erected quickly by two experienced women, and the protection it afforded was excellent. It was sturdy enough to endure the harshest winters, being waterproof and streamlined against the wind, and could be patched easily if damaged. At the top were two smoke-flaps or 'ears', each positioned by an outer pole. These ingenious yet simple devices could be positioned according to the direction and strength of the wind, preventing draughts and allowing free exit of smoke from a central fire, and thus ensuring warmth in winter. The evacuation of smoke was improved by the air currents formed between the outer cover and inner liner, and by the slight tilt of the tipi. The more acute angle of the front of the tipi also braced it against the vicious west winds of the Plains, while the smoke-flaps could be closed to allow rain to run down the outer walls. In the heat of summer the side of the tipi could be rolled up to allow ventilation.

The tipi was considered to be more than just a shelter, however, since it embodied the sacred circular form, and was seen as symbolic of the Indian's world. The painting of visionary ex-

The outside of a painted tipi; and the internal arrangements: (A) Smoke flap (B) Lodge pins (C) Smoke flap pole (D) Door flap (E) Beds (F) Fire (G) Firewood (H) Lifting pole.

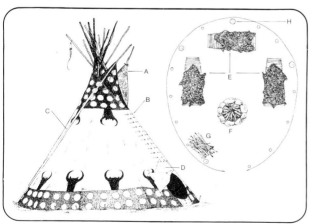

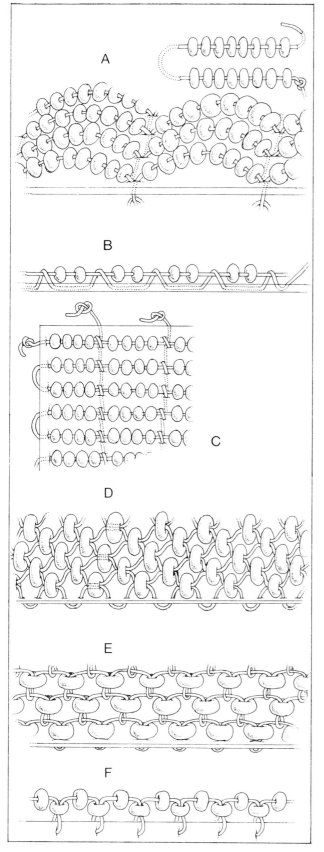

perience and war exploits on the lodge cover, door and liner was common, and made the construction of a new lodge and transfer from the old one a complex ritual.

The Plains Indians managed to live very comfortably in what we would consider cramped conditions, by enforcing strict but subtle etiquette within the tipi; walking between someone else and the central fire, for example, was thought improper. The Indians astonished some white visitors by their apparent freedom yet lack of antagonism within the lodge.

Camp Life

While it would be incorrect to see the wives of most Plains Indian men as mere chattels—and indeed, many women enjoyed a higher status than is often assumed—their society was dominated by the males. This said, however, both sexes had their own important parts to play in the prosperity and survival of the 'family, band, and tribe.

The men enjoyed greater sexual freedom than the women, and indeed boasted of their exploits, particularly those with married women. The chastity of a woman was greatly valued, however, particularly among the Cheyenne, where 'she who had yielded was disgraced forever'. A noticeably promiscuous girl's marriage prospects were very poor, while virtuous women attracted respected husbands and commanded prestigious rôles in religious ceremonies. Conversely, a prospective Tree-Notcher in the Crow Sun Dance who was not genuinely chaste had to decline the honour by declaring, 'My moccasin has a hole in it'.

Courtship was accordingly formalised to a degree, and young couples had to be wary of being seen together. Some boys made approaches when a girl went to fetch water or as she wandered with a friend through camp, but she was not often far from her grandmother's watchful eye. If a girl's parents considered her ready for marriage, they might discreetly let it be known that suitors could

Methods of beadwork: (A) Lazy stitch; covers large areas with bands of parallel rows sewn down at the ends; eight to ten beads in a row. (B) Overlaid or 'spot' stitch; two threads, one for the beads, one to attach them to the cloth; used for gently curved lines. (C) Crow stitch; rows of threaded beads secured by a second thread at right angles. (D) Netted stitch, 'gourd'; using the bead as a knot. (E) Netted stitch, 'brick'; using the looped thread as a knot. (F) Edge-beading, 'one up, one down'; many variations on this were used to edge areas of beadwork.

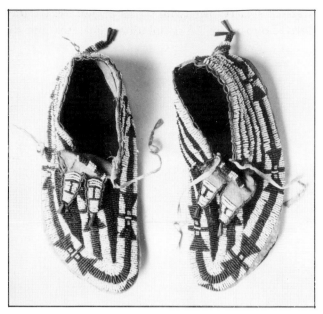

Some of the finest examples of Plains Indian beadwork are seen on moccasins. This pair are decorated with 'lazy stitch' beading in red, white, green and dark blue, the edges finished with looped trimming. Hunkpapa Sioux, collected at Fort Randall, South Dakota, 1870–80. (Berne Historical Museum)

approach. It was considered proper among many tribes for young men to cover their heads with 'courting blankets' to conceal their identity when they met the girl outside her tipi, where they embraced her with the blanket, allowing private but respectable conversation. Love-medicines and flutes also played their parts in the rituals of courting, invoking the power of animals such as the elk to inspire the faint-hearted, and to render chosen girls helpless with love.

If a suitor was encouraged by a young woman, and if his family sanctioned the match, then they would help him gather together gifts which an intermediary would take to the girl's lodge. If her family approved, they would take gifts of an equivalent value along with the bride to the boy's lodge; if not, they simply returned the original gifts. In the event of a marriage being agreed, a feast or simple ceremony set the seal on the proceedings. This was considered the honourable way to marry, although elopements were not uncommon between couples who faced opposition from their families.

Just as the relatives secured the marriage by exchanging gifts, so it was seen as a bond between families rather than simply between two individuals. Indeed, the exchange of gifts might continue for many years. One of the newly married

couple would move to the other's hunting band, and was regarded as a replacement for those members of the family unit who had themselves married into a different band. Hence the husband, in a matrilocal society, would become a member of a new unit, and would be welcomed as another provider of food and protection.

Marriage also brought taboos between the couple and their respective in-laws, usually as a sign of respect. Even before marriage, brothers and sisters were commonly kept apart from each other after a certain age despite, or perhaps because of, their closeness. After marriage, this extended to a man and his father-in-law or mother-in-law, to the extent that they were often tabooed from even looking at each other. Conversely, brothers and sisters-in-law were usually permitted a very free relationship.

A man's relations with his sister-in-law might indeed go further, since in polygamous marriages, which were quite common among many tribes, the wives were frequently sisters. A man was often considered to be under obligation to take care of his sisters-in-law if they were widowed; he might be offered his wife's sisters as wives, or might choose to ask them, since having sisters as plural wives was considered to minimise any jealousy.

Polygamy had very practical advantages for the Plains Indians. Firstly, because of the nature of this

Another fine pair of beaded moccasins, probably of Gros Ventre workmanship. (British Museum)

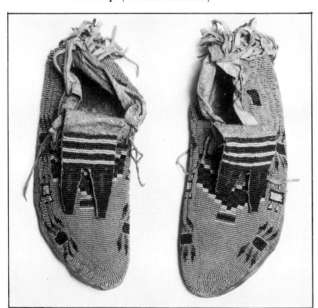

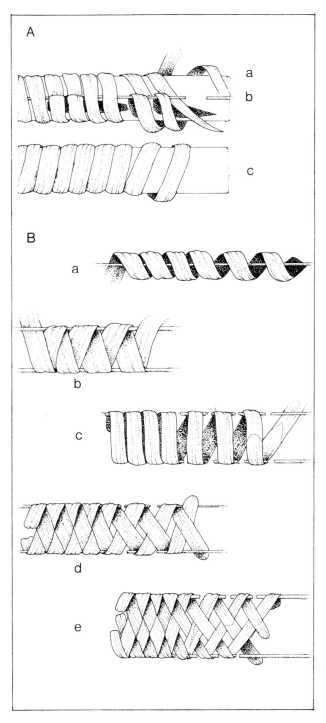

Methods of quillwork:
(**A**) *Wrapping with quills:* (**a**) **Back** (**b**) **Sinew thread which holds quill ends** (**c**) **Front.**
(**B**) *Plaiting with quills:* (**a**) **One thread and one quill sewing, creating straight or curved lines.** (**b**) **Two thread and one quill sewing, crossed sewing forming triangles.** (**c**) **Two thread and one quill straight sewing—dotted line shows how a new quill was worked in.** (**d**) **Two thread and two quill plaiting or sewing, forming small diamonds down the centre.** (**e**) **Two thread and three quill plaiting.**

warlike society, the women far outnumbered the men. To increase the population efficiently, and to replace lost warriors, polygamous marriage gave every woman an opportunity to raise children. Secondly, the chores of a prominent man's wife were arduous, and while a second wife could help maintain the lodge and prepare meals for her husband and his associates, she also provided company for the first wife while he was at war. The first wife would remain as the head of the household—she was called the 'sits-beside-me-wife' by the Blackfoot—and she would suffer no disgrace from her husband's subsequent marriages; indeed, she might even put forward the idea. For the men, plural marriage provided the potential to amass more property, since extra wives could prepare many more robes for trade, which more than compensated for the need to secure more food.

Men's and women's responsibilities and chores were clearly divided. The women, as well as raising children, were responsible for maintaining and organising the lodge, transporting it, and keeping the inside tidy. A man's wife could also be expected to help butcher the meat he had secured, to prepare his meals, and to ensure his comfort. The dressing of skins—an arduous process involving cleaning, curing, scraping and tanning of very heavy hides—again fell to the women who, moreover, had then to convert them into usable articles. Women were responsible for the intricate crafts of quilling and beading; beadwork, encouraged by the availability of trade beads, became more popular after 1830. The quality of these painstaking, decorative crafts can be seen in many artefacts such as moccasins, pipe-bags, cradles, and dresses. Proficiency in quilling and beading, and indeed in daily chores, was the women's equivalent of the men's deeds on the warpath. There were women's guilds comparable to the men's societies, such as the Quillers' Society, and prominent craftswomen attained prestige on a par with that of successful warriors.

The men's primary rôles were to feed and protect their families; and if the women's chores were more laborious, the men's were more dangerous.

The contrasting male and female rôles were developed from childhood, and children often mimicked the lives of their parents. Young girls were often given miniature tipis and dolls to look after, and imitated such things as the Scalp Dance,

Quilled deerskin shirt of Blackfoot workmanship, decorated with red and white quillwork, painted symbols and ermine fur. (British Museum)

being taught the crafts necessary for a good wife in their teens. Boys were taught to hunt and fight, and were toughened up in preparation for the fiercely competitive warrior's life that awaited nearly all of them. They were steeled for combat with vicious wrestling games, and taught the virtues of courage, while their endurance, riding and shooting skills were developed through games and guidance. Between 11 and 15 years of age they would progress from chasing calves to hunting in earnest. Finally, they would act as water-carriers in their first war-party, thus confirming the attainment of adulthood.

Hunting and the Horse

Since the Plains tribes had generally abandoned the static farming life in favour of roaming the Plains in search of game, hunting naturally formed a vital part of their lives. Even the village tribes such as the Ponca and Mandan, who subsisted mainly on their own crops, relied on the buffalo to provide meat in the summer months. Although the true nomads supplemented their diet with vegetables and berries, the bulk of their food came from hunting a wide variety of animals. Game such as the antelope and deer provided varied meat and skins; the beaver and weasel were sought for their prized fur; and birds were killed for their feathers.

Kiowa woman and baby, 1890s; the dress, moccasins and cradleboard are all typical of this southern Plains tribe. She is identified by Mayhall (see Bibliography) as Yea-Gyo-Taup, mother of Homer Buffalo.

Unquestionably, though, the staff of life for the Plains Indian was the buffalo, which was regarded as constant proof of the benevolence of the Sacred Powers. They were not only plentiful, roaming the Plains in herds of millions stretching over many miles, but also provided the Indians with more than just food. The tribes ingeniously and gratefully made use of every part of the buffalo (see accompanying diagram) to the extent that it supplied an incredible proportion of their basic needs, providing clothing, tools, shelter, fuel and food.

As the life-sustaining force, and patron of such virtues as strength and fertility, the revered buffalo was a central feature of religion. Mediums such as buffalo skulls, curiously shaped 'buffalo stones', and names derived from the animal (such as Sitting Bull) all invoked its sacred power.

Ritual also surrounded the hunting of the buffalo, with songs, dances and ceremonies assuring the successful renewal of the herds each year. One simple practice was to leave the hearts of butchered animals on the plain after a hunt, in the belief that they would replenish the herd with new life. Other ceremonies, such as the Mandan Bull Dance, symbolised the procreation of each year's calves.

Those shamans who possessed medicine derived from visions of the buffalo would be responsible for ensuring that their patron animals approached the camp. They would use their power, along with special regalia such as buffalo hoof rattles or skulls, to call the large herds to the area at times when their return was anticipated or when food was scarce. Supernatural power also extended to the actual killing of the buffalo, the appropriate shamans undergoing rituals to ensure the success of a hunt.

Various techniques were used to hunt buffalo, depending upon the time of year, and evolving with the use of the horse. Individuals or small groups sought buffalo when the hunting regulations permitted. Their prey always had to be approached from downwind, since buffalo have an acute sense of smell to compensate for their poor vision and hearing. Disguises such as wolf-skins enabled a pedestrian hunter to approach very close to a herd. The bow and arrow's silence explained its general preference over firearms, since the herd were not necessarily alarmed immediately a shot was loosed. By hunting in small groups, the hunters were also able to head off the buffaloes' retreat. In the deep snows of winter hunters on foot, sometimes using snowshoes, could drive buffalo into drifts or on to ice where their weight of up to 2,000 lbs rendered them helpless. This particular technique survived the coming of the horse, while the speed of a mounted hunter over relatively snow-free ground led to the adaption of the other individual methods of hunting.

The only way to secure a large amount of meat was through a co-operative effort. The communal drive or 'piskin' was the oldest form of group hunting, and employed all the able members of a band. The principle was to lure or drive a herd towards a corral or precipice by mimicking a calf, by enticing the leading animals, by using medicine or by sending runners behind the buffalo. The members of the band would form a long 'V', hiding themselves behind rocks or makeshift fences converging on the enclosure or escarpment. As the buffalo passed them these people leapt from hiding and began waving and screaming, spooking the herd and causing them to stampede, hopefully towards the trap. As each one leapt out the path available to the buffalo narrowed, until they realised the danger. As the leading buffalo strained to stop, they would be driven into the stockade or hurled over the cliff by the momentum of the blindly charging bulk of the herd, who would themselves have no time to stop. The stockade's entrance was usually a sharp drop or an iced-over

The uses to which the buffalo carcass was put by the Plains tribes.

(1) BEARD: Ornamentation of clothing & weapons. (2) TONGUE: Choice meat; also, hair brushes. (3) SKULL: Ceremonies, prayer, Sun Dance; tool for de-hairing rope. (4) BRAINS: Hide preparation. (5) HORNS: Cups, powder horns, spoons, ladles, quill flatteners, fire-carriers, headdresses, signals. (6) MUSCLES & SINEW: Bows (bull), thread, arrowhead and feather binding, cinches. (7) HAIR: Headdresses, saddle pad filling, pillows, rope, tipi ornaments, halters, medicine balls, bridles, weapon ornaments. (8) BONES: Knives, arrowheads, shovels and hoes, splints, sled runners, arrow straighteners, saddle trees, fleshing tools, quirts, awls, paint brushes, gaming dice. (9) TANNED HIDE: Moccasin tops, cradles, winter robes (with hair), bedding (with hair), caps and mittens (with hair), breechclouts, shirts, leggings, dresses, pipe bags, tobacco pouches and berry bags (calf hide), paint bags, quivers, tipi covers and linings, gun and lance covers, dolls, riding gear. (10) BUFFALO CHIPS (dung): Fuel, signals, ceremonies. (11) TAIL: Medicine switch, fly whisk, tipi exterior decoration, whips. (12) RAWHIDE: Containers, clothes, headdresses, parfleche, medicine bags, shields (from bull's hump), buckets, mocassin soles, rattles, drums, drumsticks, snow shoes, cinches, ropes, thongs, riding gear incl. saddles and horse shoes, knife sheaths, bull boats, quirts, belts, glue, hafting of clubs, meat and berry pounders, mauls. (13) SCROTUM: Rattles. (14) BLADDER: Sinew pouches, quill pouches, small medicine bags, food bags. (15) PAUNCH: Cooking vessel, water carrier & container. (16) MEAT: Every part eaten. (17) HOOVES: Glue, rattles.

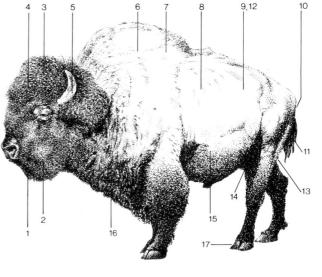

slope, preventing the buffalo from escaping the waiting hunters, while those driven over an escarpment would be killed or crippled by the fall.

The piskin was an ingenious method of compensating for the Indians' lack of mobility in pre-horse days, and could provide a huge amount of meat in return for a brief, if arduous and hazardous effort. It was unreliable, however, since the buffalo might simply never approach the area (particularly if the smell of a previous slaughter still lingered), or might suddenly veer away from the trap. It was a way of using group co-operation, and the meat was divided amongst the whole band; but its deficiencies led to the decline of the communal drive once horses became available, and only tribes poor in horses, such as the Plains Cree and Assiniboin, continued to rely on it. Most tribes evolved methods which used more fully the skills of mounted hunters, and were therefore more popular and indeed more successful.

The 'surround', which also stemmed from pre-horse days, became much easier with the advent of the horse. The principle, whether on foot or horseback, was to approach the buffalo in two lines or an arc, and then to converge on them by joining up into a wide circle and tightening it like a noose. The rather stupid animals became confused, and

The arrangement of the Cheyenne camp circle. (After Wissler)

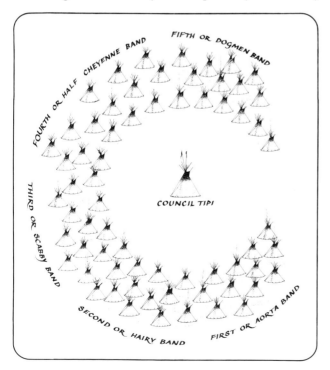

the leading buffalo would turn away from the screaming hunters and either run in circles or charge back into the centre of the herd, goring each other. The milling mass could be picked off with arrows and lances; and although the buffalo would frequently kill or injure some of the hunters, the crowding caused by the 'surround' reduced their battering-ram power, and made possible the slaughter of a large number of animals. While the 'surround' was much more practicable and efficient on horseback, it was not feasible in certain terrain, and still failed to make the best use of the horse.

The 'chase' employed the Plains riders' exceptional skills to the full. It was a straight mounted rush by the hunters from downwind of the buffalo, who would turn and flee when they realised the danger, spreading out as they ran. The cows were followed by the bulls, with the calves bringing up the rear. Unlike the 'surround', the chase made full use of the mobility of a rider, since he was free to select each individual quarry, closing on and evading the galloping buffalo as he judged best and as his skill allowed.

Once a herd had been located, the hunters approached as near as possible without disturbing the buffalo; then mounted their 'buffalo-runners', leaving common mounts with the women and children. Buffalo-runners were agile, swift and courageous horses, highly prized by their riders, and trained specifically for riding close in to the buffalo without flinching, guided only by the pressure of their rider's knees. A man's ability in the chase was only as good as his buffalo-runner, and he used this horse for nothing else.

The mounted hunters lined up equidistant from the herd, allowing all an equal opportunity, preventing individuals from scattering the herd prematurely, and ensuring the largest possible kill. At a signal the hunters charged, the superior buffalo-runners running down the cows if they were prime. As a hunter closed on his chosen target his mount brought him to the right rear flank of the buffalo in the case of a right-handed bowman, or to the left if he was a lancer. When he was as close as possible the rider released his already-nocked arrow, aiming behind the last rib of the buffalo to hit the vitals and shooting with great force, since a weak or misplaced arrow would not stop its powerful target. While some hunters employed the lance, firearms were not very effective before repeating rifles were introduced, since only these could compete with the rapid discharge accomplished by the bowman.

At the sound of the bow string, the buffalo-runner would veer away from the buffalo to evade its horns. The horse then kept pace if, as was quite common, further shots were required to complete the kill. Then the hunter would select another buffalo, repeating the process until his horse tired and the remnants of the herd outdistanced him. On average a competent man could kill two buffalo, only the supreme hunters boasting four or five of the choicest beasts.

A further advantage of using the bow was that every hunter could identify his own arrows, and claim the meat that he had killed. So, while the hunt was still a communal one, it promoted individual achievement and appealed to the Indian's competitive nature, both between hunters and in the deadly contest between man and beast.

Both men and women took part in butchering, depending upon the tribe. Animals were heavily butchered when practical and necessary, and the bulk of the meat taken back to the camp on packhorses. Raw meat was also eagerly devoured on the spot; raw liver, for example, was sometimes eaten still hot and dripping blood.

The chase naturally had its dangers, both in the possibility of a horse stumbling, and of a buffalo turning and hooking with its horns. With the increasing reliance on the horse, however, many tribes favoured this method of hunting, since it ensured that the better the combined skills of mount and rider, the greater the chance of escaping injury.

The size of a band, the distance it had to travel and its hunting methods were dictated by the availability, movement and quality of the buffalo's meat and coat. Accordingly, the life of the nomadic Indians varied with the four seasons.

During autumn, from about August to November, the tribes were dispersed into their individual bands. A band moved camp when lack of game drove them on, until their designated winter village

A northern Plains camp scene, probably Assiniboin. Of special interest is the travois and horse furniture. The travois was an essential means of transporting goods, children, or even sick adults; it was originally hauled by dogs in the pre-horse era.

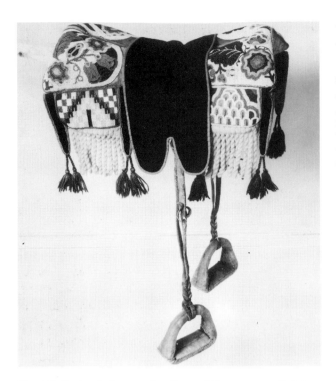

Beautifully beaded example of a saddle; museum-listed as Blackfoot, it could just as easily be Plains Cree or Chippewa. The naturalism of the motifs in the design casts doubt upon the Blackfoot identification. (British Museum)

site was reached. Individual hunting provided fresh meat throughout autumn, and around October communal hunts—usually drives until the later days—were employed to build up winter reserves from the fattened buffalo. Until the bad weather set in, the camp spent the late autumn in preparing dried meat and in obtaining and dressing hides, originally for their own lodges and clothes but in later days to supply the white traders.

During the winter months the bands sought shelter from the bitter, open Plains, and established static camps far enough apart not to deprive each other of game. Camp was only moved if a band faced starvation or needed fresh pasture, and then only if the move could be completed by nightfall. The severe weather and scarcity of buffalo, likewise dispersed into small groups seeking shelter, restricted hunting considerably. Individuals and small groups sought buffalo when the weather allowed, to supplement the dried meat supplies which were so vital when conditions confined the Indians to their lodges. The village sites were often situated near communal drives, in hope of obtaining not only precious meat, but also the shaggy winter coats of the buffalo—ideal for robes,

which were in great demand until the white man's trading season ended in about April.

When better weather heralded the arrival of spring, the bands eagerly followed the buffalo back out on to the open Plains. The richer grass ensured a plentiful supply of meat, which was generally hunted on a family basis. Communal hunts were organised when opportune; as the bands moved with the buffalo herds, so their paths crossed, so that two or three might unite in one large camp.

The only time the entire tribe or sub-tribe gathered, other than for tribal defence, was during the summer months. The bands drifted together until they were united in one spectacular camp circle; in its purest form this had the bands camped in a fixed order, as among the Cheyenne (see diagram). The summer camp was a time for reunions, affirmation of tribal unity, important councils and religious ceremonies.

While the whole tribe was together the selected warrior societies would enforce the hunt regulations, forbidding anyone to chase game outside of the communal hunts, since individuals might alert the larger herds. These regulations were very important, for although the buffalo were plentiful the tribal leaders were responsible for feeding many mouths.

The tribal hunts in the summer usually took the form of the 'surround' or the chase, and as well as food, the hunt was expected to yield sufficient tongues for the ceremonies of the Sun Dance. After the Sun Dance's conclusion, and often after a final communal hunt, the tribe would once again divide up and begin the journey towards and preparation for their winter camps.

Trade

One important offshoot from hunting was trade, both between tribes and with the whites; this was particularly so after the establishment of the white man's trading posts, of which there were approximately 150 by 1840.

Inter-tribal trade provided each tribe with variants on their own produce; the true nomads, for instance, were able to obtain maize, beans, squash and tobacco from the village tribes such as the Hidatsa, in exchange for their hunting products. Furthermore, it disseminated a related culture, associated tribes on other terms than those of war, and maintained the sign language with which the various Plains tribes could communicate even if divided by linguistic differences.

It was the trade-goods of the whites, however, which had the more acute effect on the evolution of the Plains Indians. In the 1600s the Spanish settlements in Mexico provided the first horses, while the French and English traders in the north-east began supplying the Indians with primitive firearms; and both were passed on from tribe to tribe.

The effects of the introduction of horses and firearms were dramatic. Firstly, they contributed to the migration of sedentary woodland tribes on to the Plains. In 1650, for example, the Sioux lived in the woodland Milles Lac region bordering the Plains, and only irregularly hunted buffalo. Drawn by the potential of the herds, however, and driven by their enemies the Chippewa and the allied Cree and Assiniboin—all recently supplied with firearms—the Teton Sioux moved south-west,

Pad saddle, seen from above. Made of tanned skin stuffed with deer or buffalo hair, or perhaps grass, it is decorated with quillwork in red, blue, brown, black and white. This piece is probably Sioux, pre-1837; structurally, its resemblance to a Scythian or Altai saddle found in Russia and dating from at least the 4th century BC—the dawn of military horsemanship—is quite remarkable. (Berne Historical Museum)

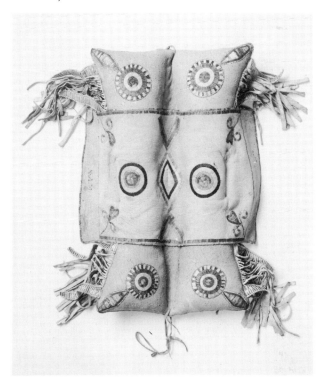

assuming their typical nomadic, buffalo hunting rôle by 1700. By 1750 they had successfully established themselves in territory west of the Missouri River.

Naturally, the life of the nomads was altered radically by the horse, which established their superiority over the sedentary tribes. The whole balance of power between the tribes was altered, while certain tribes established themselves as trading centres.

Fur companies, such as the Hudson's Bay Company established as early as 1670, continued trading with the Indians; items such as beads had a marked effect on their culture, and metal tools and utensils like kettles, knives and arrowheads eased the chores of everyday life. By 1830 the increased demand for buffalo robes meant that for the first time the Indians were—ominously—killing significantly more game than was dictated by their basic needs. Another effect was to make tribes reliant to a certain extent on the white traders, particularly as the only source of ammunition for their guns. However, one trade item which they had acquired had become so independent as to appear indigenous: and that was the horse.

The Horse

From 1600 onwards, the Pueblo Indians who worked on the Spanish ranches of northern Mexico, New Mexico and Texas gained experience in handling horses; and, through friendly contact, they passed on their knowledge to neighbouring Indians such as the Apaches. Through theft, trade, and straying from the open ranches, the horse was gradually acquired by the southernmost Indians of the Plains. The 1680 Pueblo revolt also freed thousands of mounts, and by 1700 they had spread through the Apaches to the Comanche and Kiowa, and west of the Rockies from the Ute up to the Shoshoni. By 1750 the Sioux, Cheyenne, Crow and Blackfoot all had horses, and by 1770 the diffusion was complete.

A tribe's initial reaction to the horse was one of awe, but this gave way to celebration as they realised its potential. Here was an animal with all the uses of the dog magnified by its size and temperament, which was also capable of bearing a man. The Indian names for the horse, such as 'Elk-dog', 'Sacred-dog', and 'God-dog', reflected the regard and sanctity in which they held it, as well as its size and utility.

By extending the size of their hunting grounds, the horse ushered in a period of constant tribal warfare among the Plains Indians; the new mobility of the equestrian tribes led to the repeated ousting of weaker tribes from their territories. Hunting grounds were not usually won through full-scale battles, however, but through constant harassment by raiding parties.

The 'horse raid' was not intended to be a bloody affair, but was undertaken by a small group of warriors who sought to steal the horses of their enemies by stealth. The success of such raiders represented a victory for their tribe, as well as bringing personal prestige—particularly if they escaped with the prized war or buffalo horses which were usually picketed outside their owner's tipi.

While the horse increased the danger of war simply by making war more feasible, it also heralded an age of prosperity for the Plains tribes. Only with such an efficient beast of burden could they embark with any success on a fully nomadic existence. Camp could be moved further and much more quickly, while more equipment now became manageable. Larger lodges, greater food supplies and previously inconceivable luxury items all illustrated the opportunities for wealth provided by the horse.

Indeed, the horse actually became a measure of wealth, providing material evidence of a man's prestige. The successful warrior could build up a large herd by raiding, and gained influence through the generosity he showed with his horses. Through offering them as loans and gifts the benefactor gained prestige, while the poor man was also helped. This extended to the horse being given as compensation to a wronged man, and to their being offered as gifts accompanying marriage proposals.

Clearly, then, the horse permeated every aspect of the Indians' lives. Trade, culture, leisure, hunting and war all came to revolve around it. Consequently, children were accustomed to horses from an early age; infants were carried in back-cradles while their mothers rode, and both boys and girls were capable riders by the age of seven. The boys then progressed to trick-riding; for example, a Comanche youth learned to ride bareback, and to pick up increasingly heavy weights from the ground at a gallop, in preparation for rescuing fallen comrades. Boys also tended the herds, and at an early age would be responsible for breaking horses—often in a swamp or river to discourage bucking and provide a soft landing! Throughout his life the Indian would be dependent on the horse, which even pervaded his religion. Its importance was such that it followed a prominent man to the grave, being sacrificed to accompany its rider after death as it had during life.

Naturally, the horse had an immeasurable effect on the fighting ability of the Plains Indians. Within a short time they had fully adopted a horse culture, to the extent that Indians such as the Comanche were said to be transformed from ungainliness to grace and elegance simply by mounting a horse. Logically, they also developed into fearsome fighters on horseback, the Sioux being described by Gen. George Crook of the US Army as the greatest light cavalry the world had ever known.

The mounted Indian warriors could taunt pedestrian enemies and outflank apparently superior opposition with their remarkable skills, performing such feats of horsemanship as lifting fallen comrades to the saddle, and concealing themselves by hanging below their mounts while at the gallop. Their affinity with nature and knowledge of

A wooden-framed Crow woman's saddle covered with rawhide. The pommel and cantle have a second covering of soft, tanned skin. It is decorated with pendants beaded with white, dull green, rose, and two shades of blue, on red and olive green woollen cloth. (Berne Historical Museum)

animals contributed greatly to their riding ability, superior to that of most whites; and to their immensely skilled fieldcraft, which allowed them to maximise the advantages of mounted mobility.

The horse suited the needs of the Indians so admirably and was used so effectively that it ushered in a whole new culture and lifestyle. By placing them on a much more equal footing with their environment, the horse could be said to have created, rather than just transformed, the Plains Indians.

War

While the material motives of securing favourable camp-sites and hunting grounds, and of capturing horses, contributed to tribal conflict, there were other and less obvious factors underlying the warlike nature of the Plains Indians.

Tribes sought security through aggression and self-assertion. Rather than using large numbers to destroy a weak enemy, they would instead send small war-parties into the heart of their most powerful adversary's territory. By displaying such recklessness a tribe struck at the very spirit of their enemy, while proclaiming their own strength, bravery, and—in particular—faith in their 'medicine'.

Clearly, then, an intrinsic part of war was to demonstrate complete disregard for fear, and this was well illustrated by the way in which the individual warriors fought. The actual killing of an enemy was generally secondary to displays of bravado, the greatest honour being accorded to those men who showed contempt for their adversaries, thus mirroring the tribal motives of asserting strength, superiority and the resolve necessary to survive.

War was consequently the most important sphere in which a man had to prove his worth, and the most direct way of achieving prestige. It was considered a man's business to fight, and the idea that it was 'better to die in battle than of old age or sickness' was instilled at an early age. The courting of danger brought renown, while cowardice met with scorn, and age robbed a man of his vigour and usefulness.

Because of the complex motives behind conflict

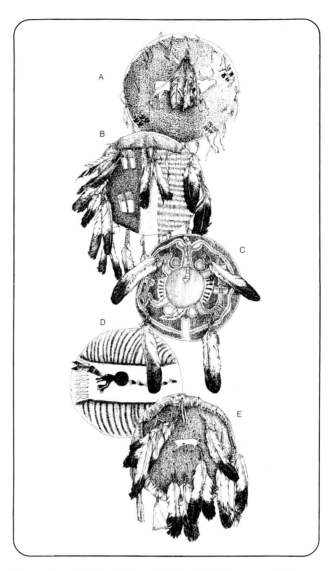

Examples of Plains Indian shields: (A) Cheyenne; this has a separate cover decorated with cow and moon symbols, hoof prints and feathers. (B) Cheyenne; painted, and decorated with cloth and eagle feathers. (C) Mandan; the painted turtle symbol stems from the owner's vision, and it is embellished with eagle feathers. (D) Crow shield with painted cover. (E) This shield is probably Sioux; it is decorated with a small painting of a bear in green, and with eagle feathers.

on the Plains, warfare took various forms. Naturally, repelling enemy attacks was one important rôle of a band's warriors, while offensive action was divided into the scalp raid and the horse raid.

Prior to the use of the horse, indecisive clashes between whole tribes exchanging arrows at long range were interspersed with more frequent, destructive attacks on small camps by superior forces. After the introduction of the horse, all raids for scalps became less frequent; while clashes of

These Northern Cheyenne warriors were photographed while working for an early 'Wild West Show' circus. Although such sources must be examined with caution, this seems to illustrate the Plains Indian warrior's costume quite faithfully.

tribal proportions between hundreds of warriors, which had sometimes included men from allied tribes, now became very rare. The scalp raid was usually launched to seek revenge on an enemy tribe, or to conclude a period of mourning. It was a highly organised affair, and consequently involved a considerable amount of ceremony. Before the raiders' departure vows and sacrifices to the Sacred Powers invoked success, while variations on the 'big' or 'horseback' dance—where the warriors donned full war regalia and paraded with their horses—aroused tribal spirit.

If the raiders—usually comprising a number of relatives of the person being mourned—returned successful, the camp would revive the ceremonies with a Scalp or Victory Dance. These dances varied from tribe to tribe, but commonly they were a celebration of the warriors' victory and bravery. Scalps were displayed on poles, often carried by the women of the camp; coups were recited, and a scalp might be presented as a replacement for the avenged camp member, an appeasement for his relatives.

The horse raid was a much more frequent and spontaneous event, often being undertaken without consultation with the band's chiefs. It became the commonest way for a man to display his courage and acquire wealth and prestige, and involved a much smaller raiding party. While the men's departure was again preceded by the invocation of 'medicine', and their successful return was cause for celebration, this was more understated than with the scalp raid, just as the raiders sought horses through silence and stealth rather than in a flamboyant clash with their enemy in a bid for scalps.

The taking of horses was not the only factor effecting a warrior's rise to prominence. While this provided him with material evidence of his exploits, the Indians also had to prove themselves by attaining other war honours or 'coups'.

The coup proper was to deliberately touch an enemy with the hand or something held in the hand—e.g. a weapon, a quirt, or a specifically-designed willow wand called a 'coup-stick'—without actually harming him. The Cheyenne warrior Yellow Nose, for example, gained great honour by snatching Custer's standard at the Little Big Horn, and using it to count coup on the enemy soldiers.

There were many other war honours which were also termed as coups, and rewarded with honorific symbols depicted on the warrior's body, clothes, horse and possessions, signifying status. Different tribes recognised different exploits as war honours, and graded them according to their worth. The Crow gave special recognition to a man who had led

A Blackfoot war shirt, collected in 1837. It is partly painted dark brown, edged with red ochre, and decorated with a large disc of orange, blue and dark brown quillwork; turquoise and white beadwork; brown human hair, and grey horse hair. Note the bear claw attached to the shoulder. (Berne Historical Museum)

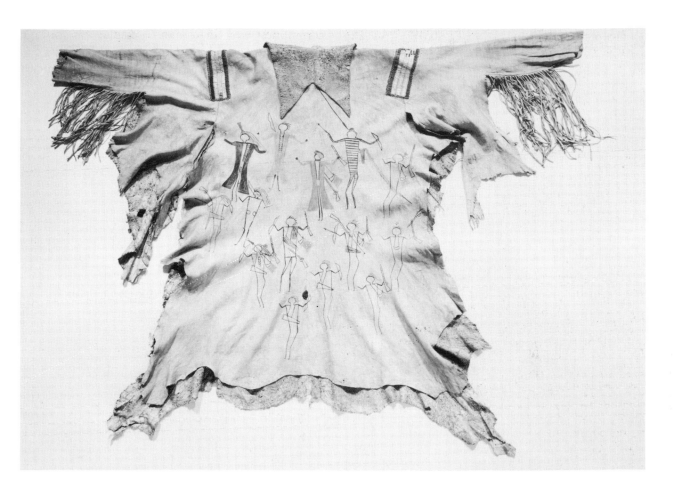

a successful raid, captured a picketed horse, counted coup, and snatched an enemy's gun. This last was considered the ultimate coup by the Blackfoot, who placed it well above the killing of an enemy, which was rated only as a minor coup by many tribes; the Assiniboin who touched a fallen enemy gained more status than the warrior who had shot him.

War exploits were also accorded varying honour depending upon their circumstances. For example, to strike a coup upon an enemy whose prowess was denoted by regalia such as a war-bonnet, or to do so actually within the enemy camp, naturally elevated the deed. Further, the first coup counted in any encounter held the greatest value; while more than one coup could be counted on the same person, the value of each diminished after the 'first coup'. The Arapaho and Sioux permitted four such coups, while the Cheyenne recognised only three.

The rewards of a notable war record were great for the Plains warrior, bringing him the right to wear specific regalia; these displayed his prowess,

A war shirt, probably Sioux, decorated with quilled and beaded bands and brown maidenhair fern. The shirt is painted front and back with stylised human figures in black, red and green. These may possibly represent warriors of other tribes killed by the shirt's owner. It is stained inside and out with red ochre. This piece dates from 1837 at the latest. (Berne Historical Museum)

and thus increased his reputation and influence. (Conversely, it was a humiliating experience for a man to have coups counted upon himself.) A proven warrior was given the honour of reciting his coups, of naming children and piercing their ears, of participating in religious ceremonies, and of progressing through the ranks of his particular warrior society.

The scalp, like a stolen horse or captured gun, also provided an individual with a trophy of war and, as proof of a killing, denoted a coup. While all tribes apart from the Cree and Sioux regarded scalping as subordinate to other coups, it was nevertheless widely practised, since a scalp was a tangible symbol of success. The hair was considered synonymous with an Indian's identity and an extension of his soul, so scalping also spiritually

85

killed a victim. This again reflected the tribal complex of self-assertion, particularly on a vengeance raid: the scalping undermined the soul of the enemy and spiritually replaced and avenged the tribe's own deceased. Scalps were flourished at Scalp Dances, and were sometimes kept thereafter, stretched across wooden hoops and decorated, for example, as powerful war medicines.

Weapons

The Plains Indians naturally possessed a wide variety of weapons, ranging from the indigenous bows, lances and clubs to the firearms and metal-bladed weapons provided by the whites.

The bow remained one of the most popular weapons from the early 'dog-days' throughout the conflict with the whites, and was used with great skill for both hunting and war. It was adapted to suit a mounted bowman by being reduced in length, to only 3 ft in some cases, making it manageable on horseback and lessening the risk of impalement in case of a fall. Bows were occasionally fashioned from horn, but more commonly from wood; this was often strengthened with strips of sinew, which was also the material for the bow-string. The making of any bow was a skilled craft, recurved bows being particularly valued for their power and beauty. Even good, straight arrows were difficult to make, and consequently were also prized. Arrowheads of bone or stone were quickly replaced by iron or steel when these became readily available from traders.

The Plains warrior's use of the bow was on a par with his mastery of the horse, and was also developed from an early age. Arrows were released with great accuracy, and enough power to go clean through a buffalo or a man's skull at close range. The Indians usually tried to close the range. Accurate at 100 yards, the bow was not effective over about 150 yards. (There have been claims for a maximum range of 300 yards under perfect conditions: this would be an astonishing performance for a bow of horseback length unless it was of composite wood/horn/sinew construction, and sharply recurved in shape.) Consequently, because the bow also had the advantages of silence and a rapid rate of discharge, it remained in full use even after the introduction of the gun.

The earliest firearms obtained by the Indians were inaccurate, slow to load and cumbersome; and while they were cheap and sturdy, their main advantages lay in their effectiveness at close range, and the initial shock and fear created by their alien appearance and effect. The typical firearms provided by the fur companies were termed 'North-West' guns, and were made by a variety of manufacturers. They were light, muzzle-loading, single-shot flintlock muskets varying from .50 to .70 in. calibre, with an enlarged trigger guard to allow firing with a mittened hand. The Indians customised their guns, shortening the barrels for ease of use on horseback, adding decoration in the form of brass studs and beautifully beaded buckskin cases, and using rawhide to repair any breakages.

Heavier, more accurate and powerful flintlock and percussion 'trade-rifles' were introduced between 1800 and 1850, but, being muzzle-loaders, these still had a low rate of fire. Consequently, while ownership of a gun was always prestigious, it was only after the 1860s, when repeating breech-loaders began to reach the tribes, that firearms began to supersede the bow. By the late 19th century, however, most warriors possessed either a rifle, such as the treasured 1866 Winchester carbine, or a pistol, the six-shot Civil War Remingtons and Colts making excellent horseback weapons for close combat.

A large number of other weapons were used, all of which were affected by the trade goods of the whites. Stone clubs were the most popular 'dog-days' weapons, and were subsequently lengthened to ease their use on horseback. At the same time the availability of metal promoted the use of other weapons, such as knife-clubs and the more common tomahawks. The very popular metal 'butcher knife' served as utilitarian tool, scalping-knife and weapon; and metal blades were used for spears and lances, in all cases replacing the laboriously crafted and fragile chipped stone heads. Lances were both weapons and symbols of office and bravery. The bow-lance, for example, was carried by Cheyenne Bowstring Society members, while many tribes used decorated staffs, often shaped like a shepherd's crook and covered in otter fur (and sometimes mistakenly called coup-sticks) to identify officers.

The shield completed the warrior's physical defences, and once again evolved with the use of the horse, being reduced from approximately 3 ft to between $1\frac{1}{2}$ and 2 ft diameter. While its construction of one or two layers of heavy buffalo hide, shrunk by heating and padded with hair or feathers, was capable of deflecting a low-velocity musket ball, much of the shield's protection was believed to lie in the 'medicine' of the designs and regalia it displayed. This decoration was believed to imbue the owner with supernatural defences, perhaps through depicting his vision-spirit—for example, by a painting of a bear claw, or the actual attachment of a real claw to the shield. A great deal of ritual surrounded the construction of a 'medicine-shield', and great care had to be taken in maintaining it. Taboos had to be observed: shields were prevented from touching the ground, and kept on tripods facing the sun to renew their power. The belief in the shield's spiritual power was such that sometimes only the thin protective cover, a miniature of the shield or a lacework shield were actually carried into battle.

Warrior Societies

Warrior societies were an important aspect of Plains life, dividing a tribe's fighting men into distinct units which provided their members with a social club, and an organisation in which they could progress through ranks of officership which brought great prestige. Each society had its own distinctive songs, dances and costume, and held regular meetings of its members. They also served the purposes of providing a policing force, encouraging bravery through inter-society rivalry, and providing a medium through which the civil chiefs and warriors could confer.

There were two distinct types of warrior society, 'graded' and 'non-graded'. The Blackfoot, Arapaho, Gros Ventre, Mandan, Hidatsa and Kiowa all used a graded system, conforming to the same general pattern. As a group of boys of a similar age became old enough to fight, they would offer a pipe and gifts to their immediate seniors, the members of the most junior society, in order to buy the right to their songs, dances, ceremonies and regalia, and consequent membership of the club. Once the sellers of membership had negotiated the maximum fee they would agree acceptance by smoking the pipe. They were then feasted by the young buyers, helped out by their relatives, while they taught them the appropriate rituals. This completed, the

This war shirt, collected in 1837, is possibly Crow. The upper part is stained with red ochre, and it is embellished with long fringes, quillwork and beadwork. (Berne Historical Museum)

new society members would proudly announce their new status. Those men who had sold them membership did not remain in the society, however; they were displaced, and subsequently sought to buy themselves into the next grade up. This process was repeated until a man sold his membership of the most senior society in the tribe, and retired as a recognised warrior.

Each society in the graded system was accorded a definite rank, so that there was no doubt as to which held greatest seniority. Since a warrior would only seek purchase into the next society when he had gained enough experience from his current fraternity, and promotion was sought by a body of men rather than an individual, the societies were approximately graded by age and achievement.

In contrast, the non-graded societies, typified by those of the Crow, Cheyenne, Sioux, Assiniboin, Pawnee and Arikara, were theoretically equivalent in status, although the popularity of each varied according to the exploits of its members. The societies did not generally discriminate between those wishing to join their ranks, since a substantial membership was important for the club's survival. Those warriors whom the society thought would improve their status were lured by gifts, while a man's relatives often affiliated themselves to his society. Occasionally a warrior would change societies either to replace a dead relative, or in the case of a disagreement. Because there was no formal grading of clubs inter-society rivalry was intense, with each vying for superiority. The Crow Lumpwood and Fox clubs took this to extremes, practising the formalised abduction of each other's members' wives. The fierce rivalry thus engendered was carried on to the battlefield, where each society strove to strike the first coup, and its members fought fearlessly out of duty towards their fraternity.

The duties of the graded and non-graded societies were very similar, and both were divided up into various honorary ranks. These offices were often two-sided, for while they conferred great honour, they also usually demanded some personal sacrifice or commitment. For instance, a 'bear-belt wearer' in the Big Dog Society of the Crow would pronounce his status by wearing a belt of bearskin complete with claws, by daubing his body with mud, and by rolling up his hair into tight balls imitating a bear's ears. While such an officer would receive privileges, such as eating first at a feast, acceptance of the rank would also entail the commitment to walk straight up to the enemy, regardless of safety; never to retreat; and to rescue any tribesman in danger.

Similar vows were common for both individuals and particular societies. Such warriors as the members of the Kiowa Koitsenko or Ten Bravest, and certain members of the Miwatani or Tall Ones of the Sioux and the renowned Cheyenne Dog Soldiers—all élite societies pledging unflinching bravery—would wear a sash which they staked to the ground in battle. There they would fight until victory or death, unless a fellow society member pulled up the stake and released them from their vow.

Perhaps the most extreme examples of reckless-ness were the 'contrary' warriors, who pledged themselves—out of grief, or foolhardiness, or in accordance with a vision of the much feared Thunder—to behave inversely, saying and doing everything opposite to the norm. Contrariness was a recurrent theme in Plains religion—the Blackfoot Sun Dancer, for instance, received cuts in his skin of the opposite depth to that which he had requested—and, similarly, the contrary warrior was believed to possess great power.

The Cheyenne had particular warrior societies for the contraries, such as the Bowstring Society; such men were formidable enemies, since, confident of their power and burdened by the restrictions of their rôle, they fought without fear. They would refrain from joining battle if victory was inevitable, charging in to fight ferociously only when their comrades were defeated. The Crow 'crazy dogs wishing to die' actively sought their own deaths.

Going to the opposite extreme, a man could opt out of the military scheme altogether, becoming a 'berdache' or transvestite. Such a decision stemmed from a vision in which a boy was offered the choice of a bow or pack strap by the Moon, and was handed the pack strap if he hesitated, thus symbolising his feminised future. Upon reaching manhood he would follow his nature and begin dressing, speaking and behaving as a woman. Like the contraries, berdaches both suffered ostracism and enjoyed power. Their effeminacy made them popular as matchmakers, and they were also sought-after to accompany war parties, both for their medical skills and because they were believed to bestow strength and virility upon the fighters. The berdaches also suffered scorn, however, since they represented the complete opposite of the 'fearless warrior' ideal.

War Costume

While a certain basic wardrobe was reserved simply for everyday comfort, the Plains warrior also wore highly decorative dress or war costume for ceremonies, parades, burial and battle, with embellishments which served various purposes. Firstly, display costume could denote society or

A buffalo skin robe of Mandan workmanship, pre-1837. It is decorated with a circular presentation of a war bonnet in black, surrounded by pictographs of deeds of war—possibly those of the Mandan chief Mato-tope. (Berne Historical Museum)

tribal rank, or membership of a visionary cult. Secondly, designs reflected visionary experience and consequently invoked 'medicine', providing supernatural guidance and protection. Thirdly, war costume displayed achievement marks, retaining and proclaiming evidence of a warrior's accomplishments.

The war shirt or 'scalp shirt' provides a good example of all three functions. In early years it was almost exclusively worn as a badge of office; this is most clearly illustrated by the leaders of the Sioux, who were called Shirt-Wearers, each being presented with a painted shirt fringed with hair symbolising the people they were responsible for. Prominent warriors, when they wore scalp-shirts as marks of distinction, fringed the neck and sleeves either with hair taken from an enemy or—particularly among the Blackfoot and Crow—with ermine pendants. Bands of beadwork or quillwork along the arms and over the shoulders, or in the form of rosettes, also denoted military excellence; among the Crow, for example, four such bands symbolised a holder of the four main coups.

War shirts were also decorated with painted representations of exploits, the symbols for different coups varying from tribe to tribe. Some commonly used designs were a hand, representing success in hand-to-hand combat; stripes, which could symbolise wounds or coups; pipes, numbering the war-parties led; and hoofmarks, indicating numbers of horses captured.

While a war shirt could therefore provide a pictographic record of the wearer's coups, it also offered him supernatural protection through other designs and trimmings. Such shirts, which might form a vital part of a man's war medicine, sometimes offered protection by association with the danger: for example, by depicting black dots or 'tadpoles' which supposedly made the wearer immune to bullets. Alternatively, shirts were painted with designs of a natural helper seen by the wearer in a vision, such as the bear or eagle, which could impart protection from the Sacred Powers. Pierced shirts were also worn as supernatural defences.

Shirts were not the only items of costume which were important for their decoration. Coups and medicine beliefs were also represented on robes, leggings and moccasins. The large surface area of

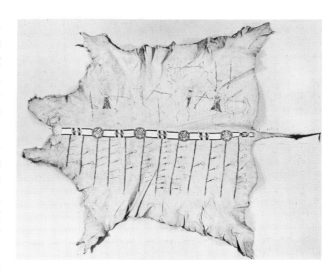

Buffalo robe, decorated from head to tail with a broad band and rosettes of quill- and beadwork. Above the band pairs of fighting men are painted in red and black; below it are 12 parallel lines with a series of symbols. (Berne Historical Museum)

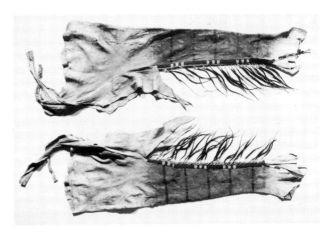

A Blackfoot man's leggings. The top half of each is stained with red ochre, the lower part dark brown with five horizontal brown stripes painted on. Beaded strips, predominantly turquoise blue with white stripes, are sewn down the length; and the fringing is of scalp locks of dark brown human hair.

robes was ideal for detailed pictographs; while leggings were fringed with hair in the same way as shirts, as well as painted with protective and honorific designs such as stripes. Moccasins were beaded with various intricate designs, and were also fringed; a Crow coup striker, for example, wore wolf tails at his heels.

Full costume was undoubtedly worn into battle, and not just reserved for ceremonial occasions. Warriors carried it until the enemy were sighted; then they would generally prepare for battle by donning their war costume, preparing any other regalia, applying face and body paint, and even

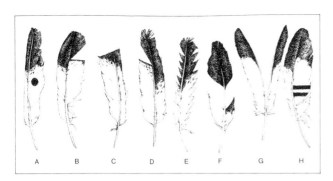

Examples of feather 'heraldry'. This varied considerably from tribe to tribe; besides various different ways of cutting or painting the feather, the type of feather and the position in which it was worn were also significant. (A) With red spot—'killed an enemy'. (B) 'Killed an enemy and took his scalp'. (C) 'Cut an enemy's throat'. (D) 'Third coup'. (E) 'Fourth coup'. (F) 'Fifth coup'. (G) 'Has been wounded many times'. (H) Two red stripes—'third coup'.

rebraiding their hair. The reasons for such preparation were quite complex. Firstly, according to the Cheyenne warrior Wooden Leg, warriors dressed for death, just as they did when seriously ill. Secondly, the preparations for battle, performed with appropriate ceremony, put the warrior in touch with the sources of supernatural power, his regalia reminding him constantly of his spiritual obligations. Finally, a warrior's dress reflected his intentions and status, displaying his proven strength and courage, and asserting his confidence and superiority. Those warriors, therefore, who chose to fight virtually naked neither feared death nor needed physical protection, since they were convinced that their charms, paint and prayer fortified them against the enemies' weapons.

Naturally, the importance of costume extended to weapons and accessories. Again, coups were denoted, particularly by painting weapons; the Mandan chief Four Bears wore a red-painted knife in his hair and carried a lance of the same colour to symbolise that he had killed with those weapons. Status was signified by society lances and sashes, while medicine was also invoked, most obviously by the designs on shields but also by the use of special weapons, such as the Blackfoot knife set into a bear-claw hilt. Warriors also wore or carried objects which had a purely spiritual purpose. These 'war medicines' took various forms, from the popular leather pouch containing symbols of a warrior's power, to dolls, pendants, pipes, hoops and feathers. Such items were fixed to shields, worn around the neck or in the hair, carried, or possibly left in camp if

their nature was such that simple ownership conferred power. Reliance on them was great, whether they were an individual's personal talismans or those of the leader or 'pipe-holder' of a war-party. The warriors would smoke the leader's pipe and meditate upon his medicine to invoke its guidance, as well as following their own rituals, culminating in the ceremonial preparation for combat.

A warrior's apparel was usually completed by paint, and feathers worn in the hair. Systems of feather heraldry were employed by the Sioux and such tribes as the Hidatsa, Crow, Gros Ventre, Mandan and Assiniboin. Plumes from birds of prey, particularly the brown-tipped white feathers of the immature golden eagle, were cut, painted and positioned on the head (see diagram) to denote coups in the same way as the symbols used on costume. The specific meanings of different feather designs varied from tribe to tribe, and between individuals.

While any warrior could wear feathers, the right to wear an eagle feather war bonnet was earned only by a few. A warrior would first put on the bonnet either when he himself felt worthy of it or at the urgings of his superiors. To do so was a

Arapaho war bonnet, once owned by Yellow Calf. (British Museum)

First half of 19th century:
1: Hidatsa 'Dog-Soldier'
2, 3: Assiniboin warriors

A

Blackfoot:
1: Motokiks women's society member
2: Blood warrior
3: Warrior in winter dress
4: Elder

B

Blackfoot:
1: Mother with child
2: Grandmother
3, 4: Minipoka

C

D

Arapaho:
1: White Woman
2: Ghost Dancer, 1890

Kiowa and Comanche:
1: Kiowa brave
2: Kiowa woman
3: Comanche brave
4: Comanche girl

F

Little Bighorn, 25 June 1876:
1: Cheyenne brave
2: Buffalo Calf Road Woman
3: Crow scout

G

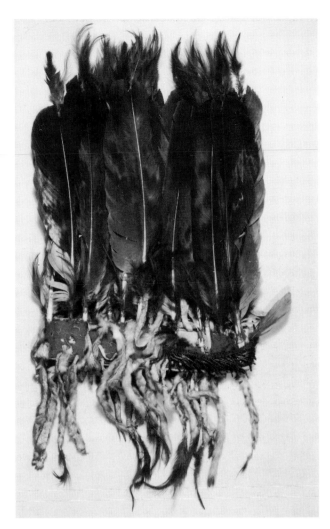

Blackfoot straight-up headdress—see Plate B4. (British Museum)

profession of his belief in his own fighting ability, and an assumption, therefore, of great responsibility. A bonnet-wearer claimed to be one of his tribe's ablest defenders, and as such he was expected to set an example of bravery, despite being an obvious target for enemy coup-seekers. The feathers in war bonnets were symbolic of coups among those tribes practising heraldry, and flags bearing further plumes also symbolised the carrier's bravery as well as providing a rallying point for fellow warriors.

Headdresses, sometimes centred on stuffed birds, were also worn as medicine items or to signify membership of a society, the members of the Miwatani Society wearing bonnets of eagle-owl feathers.

Face and body paint established the Indian in the rôle of a warrior. While certain colours could have specific meanings (black, for instance, often signifying victory), and while coup marks were used and old wounds highlighted, a warrior's war paint designs were usually only significant to him. Together with solemn prayers and vows, and the warrior's sacred costume and regalia, these designs completed the medicine preparations which fortified him for war.

Religion, Ceremony and Medicine

The Plains Indians believed that supernatural power pervaded every aspect of their life, and that to live in harmony with it was necessary to survival. This abstract force embraced all the natural mysteries of the Plains, so that not only their world but the very life the Indians led was considered sacred, and consequently their religion was a very real and practical belief.

A manifestation of spiritual power was called 'maxpé' by the Crow and 'wakan' by the Sioux, who therefore called a holy man a 'Wicasa-Wakan', and their supreme deity 'Wakan-Tanka' or the Great Spirit. 'Wakan' power was the source of what came to be known as medicine, so that 'making medicine' simply meant invoking the Sacred Powers. Medicine was sought and held through prayer, self-induced visions, ritual, and medicine items such as pipes and other bundles. It was so important because it provided for the tribe, and guided warriors and healers. The sacred right to invoke medicine had to be attained and preserved; and the life-sustaining force of the tribe, both in the abstract and in matters of material subsistence such as the buffalo, had to be renewed regularly.

The structure of the Indians' deities was complex, often loosely defined, and varied from tribe to tribe. A belief in a dominant force or supreme deity, the original source of medicine and controller of lesser spirits, was widespread. The lack of clarity that surrounded this being lay in the belief that it was both personified as a distinct Great Spirit, while also being seen as a part of everything, an omniscient force. The Cheyenne beliefs typify this, since while they recognised Ma'heo'o as the 'All-Father', their cosmology incorporated a group of subordinate deities emanating from the 'All-Father'. While these had distinct identities they could also be seen collectively as a single entity, 'Ma'heono', the Sacred Powers. Since medicine lay in all things, everything, including these Sacred Powers, was a part of the Great Spirit, whose power divided and sub-divided indefinitely.

The sun was generally the most powerful subsidiary power, the bringer of light and life. It was distinct from the Great Spirit, but they were closely integrated, since tribes commonly regarded the sun as a material token of the Great Spirit's existence. While the supreme deity was an abstract, the sun was a visible symbol, and the tipi was always pitched to face east so that prayers of thanks could be offered up to it at the beginning of each day.

The moon, sky and Earth were also venerated, as were the stars, the Morning and Evening Stars playing a large part in Pawnee ceremony. The Sacred Powers were commonly divided into two groups, the Cheyenne for instance recognising the Listeners-Above dominated by the sun, and the Listeners-Below dominated by the Earth. This idea of opposites, be they above and below, good and evil, male and female, was a consistent theme in the Plains religions; the Indians attempted to balance them, engendering power through harmony.

There were a number of other recurrent themes which reflected the constancy of religion. Tribal sites of great spiritual importance were common, usually isolated summits or places of natural wonder where medicine was most effectively sought through visions. To the Comanche, Medicine Bluff in the Wichita Mountains was important, while the Cheyenne called Bear Butte the Sacred Mountain, believing it to be the place where the All-Father met with their prophet Sweet Medicine, and the source of medicine on Earth.

The sacred circle, as the perfect form and the shape of natural phenomena such as the sun, was represented by the camp circle, the base of the tipi, and the performance of ceremonies in a clockwise, circular direction where possible, reflecting the movement of the sun. It was also divided by the sacred number four into the continuous life-pattern, at the semi-cardinal directions in the case of the Cheyenne. South-east represented renewal, south-west growth and nourishment, north-west maturity, and north-east completion of, and return along, the unbroken circle to renewal. This explains the importance of renewal in many ceremonies, as well as the emphasis placed on the number four. There were the Sacred Powers of the Four Winds and the Four Directions, and the number was also believed to permeate everything natural. Consequently, crosses were worn to symbolise the Four Directions, and the number figured significantly in ritual, ranging from four objects being used, to three feints being made before a movement was completed.

The Vision Quest

The Indians believed that to distinguish themselves, and indeed to survive, they needed to acquire medicine from the Sacred Powers through visionary experience. Dreams came to the fortunate involuntarily when they were children, and as they grew up further knowledge revealed the full extent of their blessing. Most, however, had to reach out

Oglala Sioux 'trailer' war bonnet from the Pine Ridge Reservation in South Dakota. (Berne Historical Museum)

for power, invoking the aid of the Great Spirit through self-sacrifice. Usually, as a boy approached manhood, he would seek out a shaman to instruct and assist him in his 'vision quest', and together they decided the time and method of the youngster's undertaking.

To begin with, the vision-seeker would usually purify himself in a 'sweat lodge', a low dome of willow saplings covered with skins to retain the scorching vapours given off by water poured on to red-hot rocks placed in a central pit. Sage was also burnt or rubbed on the body, and paint applied in sacred designs.

The vision quest itself was endured in a place of solitude, allowing the vision-seeker to concentrate fully upon the Sacred Powers. The actual form it took varied, but it usually involved the vision-seeker remaining alone in the same spot for an agreed number of days and nights, perhaps broken up by visits from his supervising shaman. Some would sit in the darkness of a small lodge, some would remain unsheltered, while others stood in one spot staring at the sun to force themselves to stay awake. Sioux vision-seekers paced out a cross from a central pole to poles marking the Four Directions, hung with offerings of tobacco and red flannel strips.

The vision-seeker was naked apart from perhaps a breechclout and moccasins, and shunned all earthly protection other than a buffalo robe for warmth at night. Sacred objects such as a buffalo skull, sage, and buffalo chips were used to forge a link with the Sacred Powers, as was a pipe, which carried the prayers of the vision-seeker to the Great Spirit. Food and drink were abstained from for the duration of the quest, so that, with his mind resting inexorably on the Great Spirit, the vision-seeker, weak from hunger and thirst, might achieve a vision. Some attempted to accelerate the effect through self-sacrifice, chopping off a finger joint, for instance, offering up their very flesh to the Great Spirit, as well as weakening themselves through loss of blood and so encouraging a trance.

Those who failed to see a portent of their medicine either resigned themselves to failure or prolonged their ordeal. Weak and alone, the successful vision-seekers would either see or hear a sign of their medicine while conscious, or, semi-conscious, they would drift from fitful sleep into a trance revealing a vivid apparition. Some fainted

Little Wolf, Sweet Medicine Chief of the Cheyenne; and, seated, Morning Star (Dull Knife), Chief of the Northern Cheyenne, photographed during a delegation to Washington in 1873. (Smithsonian Institution, courtesy Robin May)

from lack of food, drink, sleep, or blood, and discovered spiritual help when close to death.

The actual visions which men saw were obviously very varied, but as the power of the Great Spirit was believed to be diffused throughout the Indians' natural surroundings, it was in a comprehensible, natural form that medicine was most often revealed, the commonest visions being of birds and animals. Birds could impart the powers which were characteristic of their own abilities, from the arrogant, ferocious skills of the eagle, through the agility of the kingfisher, to the knowledge and acute hearing of the tiny chickadee. Animals provided medicine in the same way, the buffalo, for example, signifying hunting success or abundant food, or imparting its powers of strength and tenacity.

Birds and animals, as well as being able to impart abilities to the dreamer in their own right, might also be seen as messengers from the Sacred Powers, the owl, for example, sometimes being seen as a servant of the moon.

Thus a vivid dream of an encounter with, or even the distant sound of, a bird or animal might fulfil the vision-seeker's quest, assuring him of a natural medium through which to attain his medicine by providing him with a personal supernatural guardian or 'vision spirit'. Alternatively, the vision-seeker might see himself, displaying his medicine by his actions. He could be wearing special clothing or paint and riding a horse bearing painted symbols, while displaying invulnerability by riding through a hail of bullets, arrows, or even lightning bolts. An animal guardian might also be revealed through some adornment, such as a bear claw necklace; or by a natural power, such as the eagle, saving him from danger.

A vision had to be interpreted before it could be fully understood, so the visionary would receive instruction from his tribe's shamans, or possibly from a 'dream cult'. These comprised a small membership who had all seen the same vision spirit, and could share and represent their medicine collectively, while enhancing their prestige. Each cult developed specific ceremony and regalia derived from the appearance and actions of their supernatural patron; thus Bear Cult members mimicked the bear, invoking medicine known to provide guidance in both war and doctoring.

The relationship between a visionary and his vision spirit can be seen in the sense of an adoption. The vision spirit would direct its spiritual son in the use of its imbued power, outlining the necessary ritual, paint, song, dress and taboos. An intrinsic idea underlying this was that medicine was a tangible substance which was transferable, from the Sacred Powers to nature, from nature to the

Indians, and subsequently from one man to another. The vision spirit was regarded as having offered a part of itself to the visionary, a share in its personal medicine. The rest of the visionary's life was then spent under a spiritual protection and obligation, fulfilling the requirements of his vision.

Initially, he secured his relationship with the Sacred Powers by forming his acquired medicine into a palpable object, called a 'medicine bundle'. This could take many forms, from an actual bundle of talismans to charms centred around a pipe; even a medicine shield was a form of 'bundle'. Derivatives from this included necklaces, clothing, feathers, adornments hung from shields, small medicine pouches and even the paint a man wore, all of which, along with appropriate ritual, invoked and retained a man's medicine. Often they worked through association, so that medicine acquired from the eagle might be represented by an eagle skin bundle containing charms outlined in the vision, an eagle feather worn in the hair, a single talon pendant hung around the neck, and a complete claw attached to a painted shield.

Subsequent meditation and ritual provided receptive visionaries with medicines from different sources; for instance, Weasel Tail of the Blood Blackfoot possessed a wide variety of medicines, regarding the otter, king-bird, and weasel all as personal helpers, and consequently owning a complex range of bundles. Provision was also made, however, for those men who failed to achieve a vision. Since medicine was transferable, they were able to purchase a share of power from a more fortunate visionary, who would assume the paternal rôle in the standard adoption.

Certain men and women received visions of particular spiritual significance, which portended a future as a shaman. Such visions were usually distinguishable by the fact that rather than simply offering power, they also conferred a degree of understanding. This ranged from the visionary being taught the use of certain herbs in healing, to his being made aware of the sacred nature of the world. The Sioux Black Elk was shown by the Sacred Powers that 'the sacred hoop of my people was one of many hoops that made one circle'; and in such a way was given a comprehension of spiritual matters.

The main distinction made between shamans

(A) Sioux tomahawk pipe (B) Crow medicine pipe (C) Northern Plains pipe dating from after 1850 (D) Crow sacred pipe, c.1850

was that between priests and doctors. Doctors were those shamans who used their supernatural power, possibly together with herbal remedies and rites learnt from their elders, to heal. A priest was a spiritual advisor and interpreter. Taught through study under an experienced holy man, and sanctioned by visionary experience, he was responsible for the preservation of tribal lore, relics and ceremony, and for the direction of spiritual affairs.

One important rôle played by the priests was that of ritual keepers of the tribal bundles. These were medicines of tribal, rather than individual significance, exemplified by the huge Beaver Bundle of the Blackfoot. This was the largest of all tribal bundles, symbolising nearly all birds and animals through the numerous skins it contained, as well as being the 'father' of the other Blackfoot bundles, since it also held aspects of each of them. It originated from the Beaver, who taught the first keeper the sacred songs which accompanied the bundle's ceremonies; and since it was very sacred, the keeper's rôle was equally revered. His spiritual obligations were to memorise the ceremonies and songs (originally over 400 of them) to conduct the rituals and maintain the bundle, to possess the knowledge of the associated medicines, and to live a life in harmony with nature. The Beaver Bundle was opened to offer a general blessing, as part of tribal ceremonies of renewal and to overcome illness and hunger. The keeper also used its potent medicine to predict the

The integrity of the US Government's reservation agents varied sharply. Some were well-meaning men doing their best under difficult circumstances; others were out-and-out swindlers, who did not care whether their Indians lived or died so long as their own opportunities for corruption were undisturbed. This photo shows an Indian agent with Arapaho braves.

weather and guide camp moves, and kept a calendar and recorded the 'winter counts' which formed the tribal history.

Tribal bundles, like all medicines, could be transferred. This was usually done formally, the keeper's neophyte inheriting the bundle and its obligations following years of study, thus ensuring its continued blessing upon the tribe. The old-time transfer of the Sacred Arrows of the Cheyenne entailed the new keeper—as a sign of his dedication to the Great Spirit or All-Father, and in appeal for His blessing—offering up numerous slices of his own flesh cut in sacred patterns, the scars of which remained for life.

The Sun Dance

Since their religion was such a constant practice, continuous acknowledgement of the Sacred Powers being important to maintain harmony, various simple forms of worship permeated the Indians' everyday lives.

Prayers and offerings were constantly offered up to the Sacred Powers. At their simplest they involved thanksgiving to the sun and the Great Spirit, or the offering of a morsel of food to the Sky and Earth; but they also extended to pledging a

Shun-ka Blo-ka or 'He-Dog' of the Oglala Sioux. It is said that when Crazy Horse and his followers surrendered at Camp Robinson on 6 May 1877, He-Dog placed his scalp shirt on Lt. W. P. Clarke to signify that war between them was at an end. (Smithsonian Institution, courtesy Robin May)

sacrifice of possessions, participation in a ceremony, or sacrifice of a man's flesh in exchange for safety or success in war or recovery from illness.

The smoke from a pipe carried prayers to the Sky, Mother Earth and the Four Directions, while the sacred number, circle and sunwise direction all provided a constant means of demonstrating awareness of spiritual obligations. The rituals that surrounded sacred objects were consistent with this. The ceremony that surrounded the opening of a medicine bundle, for instance, or the taboos that accompanied the use of medicine items, ensured careful observance of their sanctity.

The culmination of these rituals were the tribal ceremonies, the most important of which was the Sun Dance. This was a major tribal ceremony of all of the typical Plains tribes, apart from the Comanche, until 1874. It was held when the whole tribe was camped together—sometimes annually, as among the Blackfoot, and sometimes sporadically, as with the Crow. Since tribes formed the Sun Dance into a composite of their other ceremonies

there were obviously tribal variations, but as it had been diffused from tribe to tribe there were also common features.

Primarily, the ceremony allowed the tribe as a whole to supplicate the Sacred Powers, while different tribes also had other distinct motives. To the Crow, it was a means of securing a vision promising revenge; to the Cheyenne, a ceremony of renewal. Underlying these tribal motives was the contractual vow taken by the central 'pledger' to sponsor the ceremony in exchange for divine favour, be it a safe return from war or recovery from illness. Similar vows, either taken for themselves or for relatives, also bound individuals to more minor rôles. Women always either assumed the rôle of central pledger—illustrated by the Sun Dance of the Blackfoot, which centred on a woman's purchase of the valuable Nataos Bundle and sponsorship of the ceremony—or at least played an important part.

The sacred number four was recurrent, this number of days often being set aside both for the preparatory ceremonies—illustrated by the 'Lone Tipi' rites of the Cheyenne—and for the main rituals of the Sun Dance. These were initially focused on the construction of the medicine lodge, a large building which housed the concluding ceremonies, situated in the middle of the camp circle and centred on a significant central pole.

The finding of a forked cottonwood tree suitable for this task involved a great deal of ritual, since the tree was treated as being symbolic of an enemy. Consequently, a privileged scout would usually be sent out to find it; and following his return to report the successful discovery of an enemy, the cottonwood was ceremonially 'killed' and coup counted on it. Some tribes, such as the Crow, reserved the right to notch the tree, before it was felled, for a virtuous woman.

When the central pole had been carried back to camp it was raised at the centre of the lodge. For the Blackfoot this completed the central pledger's rôle as she ended her fast, the cottonwood proclaiming her virtue if it was raised perfectly upright. The central pole remained steeped in symbolism, particularly the bushy fork at its top, which was seen by some tribes as the nest of the Thunderbird, and was commonly hung with offerings, for instance of tobacco or cloth. The pole was also usually hung

A Sioux warrior. Note the broad beaded strip on the blanket worn wrapped around the waist, and the breast plate of bone 'hair-pipes'.

the Buffalo Dance, the ritual killing of one or two buffalo, and the very important preparation and solemn consumption of the sacred buffalo tongues.

The most spectacular element of the Sun Dance was the self-torture of dancers who had pledged to offer their flesh in supplication of the Sacred Powers. While some men—such as the Blackfoot Weather Dancers, the Crow central pledger, and the Sioux first grade dancers—performed an arduous dance, bobbing up and down on their toes, blowing on an eagle-bone whistle, and staring at the Sun or central pole, others had the flesh of their breasts and backs pierced through by skewers.

Some attached these to buffalo skulls, which they dragged until the skewers broke free or they had walked a certain distance. Others were attached to poles and fell back on the skewers, which tore their flesh; while some, such as the highest grade of Sioux dancers, were actually suspended from the central pole by ropes to the skewers through their breasts, until the skewers broke free. The loose skin was cut off and placed at the central pole as a sacrifice to the sun.

Clearly, such participants in the Sun Dance made very receptive visionaries. (Their attendants sometimes unwittingly planted the skewers so deeply that the dancers could only tear them free if others jumped on them to add their weight.) The achievement of a vision by the central pledger was a necessary condition for the ending of the Crow Sun Dance. The self-torture dancers offered the ultimate sacrifice to the Sacred Powers, and demonstrated unquestioning faith in their religion, while completing the ceremonies, which served to unite the tribe in worship, and to renew their dedication for the year ahead.

with effigies of some form. The Sioux painted it at the Four Directions, and hung up rawhide figures of the Whirlwind and Crazy Buffalo, two evil spirits who were later shot down by the tribe's warriors. The Crow and the Kiowa focused their ceremonies on a doll fixed to the central pole, the Kiowa using their sacred Tai-me doll, while an effigy was also contained in the Blackfoot Nataos Bundle head-dress.

A great number of ceremonies, usually preceded by fasting and purification rites by the important participants, were held around the central pole. There was dancing by both the men's and women's societies, as well as the recounting of coups by the tribe's warriors. An altar was always prominent, playing a central rôle in the Cheyenne ceremony as its construction symbolised the renewal of the Earth, and was commonly adorned with the painted skull of a buffalo. This sacred animal was also represented by such aspects of the Sun Dance as

Conquest

The 1851 Laramie Treaty attempted to resolve the fundamental problem of the increasing number of troops, traders, settlers, prospectors and other emigrants who were crossing and consequently destroying the ancestral homelands of the Plains nations. By offering material compensation to tribes in exchange for their acceptance of previously inconceivable boundaries and the establishment of roads and forts, the treaty provided an obviously temporary solution. It was one in a series of agreements which failed or were broken, usually by the whites. In this case matters came to a head when US Army Lt. Grattan and his 30-man party were killed while impetuously and illegally attempting to arrest a Sioux warrior.

Years of alternating conflict and truce followed, resulting from a fundamental clash of cultures. The expanding, materialist society of the whites claimed land that was considered sacred by a spiritual people, and attempted to confine the essentially nomadic Plains Indians to ever-smaller territories. The defiant defeat of Gen. Custer at the Little Bighorn in 1876, by a force comprising mainly Sioux and Cheyennes, only served to provoke an increasingly ruthless campaign by the US Army.

One reason for the futility of the Indian cause was that they were divided by tribal feuds; Custer, for example, was guided to the Little Bighorn by Crow and Arikara scouts. A united Indian nation could have defended their lands more ably, but, in the words of Sitting Bull, they were 'an island of Indians in a lake of whites'.

This proud leader of the Hunkpapa Sioux had offered his blood to the Great Spirit by scarifying his arms, and performed the gazing-at-the-sun dance, to augur Custer's defeat, while at the same time prophesying that desire for the whites' goods would 'prove a curse to this nation'.

His warning was perceptive, for it was not only through war that the Plains Indians were defeated. Trade goods had established a certain Indian dependence on the whites, while also exposing them to the sad effects of alcohol, against which they had an unusually low tolerance. Foreign diseases such as smallpox, against which the Indians had no natural defences, wiped out whole bands at a time; while the destructive nature of the whites also took its toll through the callous slaughter of the buffalo herds. Following the Indians' considerably increased hunting efforts to meet trade demands, white professional hunters arrived by the 1860s. They left most of the meat from their kills rotting on the Plains, while securing so many hides that they disturbed migration patterns as well as reducing the buffaloes' overall numbers drastically. Some Army officers were well aware that by destroying their staff of life they were destroying the Plains Indians.

The most superficial comparison of white and Indian cultures shows us that the destruction of the latter was inevitable. Apart from the sheer numbers involved, and the whites' technological advantages; apart from the growing Indian dependence on white goods, and the parallel destruction of the buffalo herds which were the material basis of their lifestyle; apart from all these weaknesses, the Indians also suffered fatally when their attitude to warfare was confronted by the European military tradition of the whites.

The red man was the individual warrior supreme, and his courage, endurance, horsemanship and fieldcraft brought him many victories over the whites: but almost always on a strictly limited, local scale. It was almost unknown for the Indians to assemble an 'army' large enough to threaten seriously a major US column in pitched battle— thus the extraordinary trauma caused by the Custer massacre. It was terribly difficult for the Indians to hold such a force together in the field for more than a few weeks. The Plains warrior was, as we have seen, a hunter and provider too—war was only one facet of his life. The white trooper might be individually less impressive as a fighting man; but his dogged, plodding columns did not dwindle and drift apart as the riders became bored, tired, disheartened, or worried about their families. The trooper was the tool—in theory, and usually in practice—of a single overall command with a unified plan of campaign. The Indians, as we have seen, were always weakened by a disunity which must seem chronic to white eyes. But this is to misjudge the Indians—to apply to them, with hindsight, the military thought-patterns of an alien culture. Their disunity was not frivolous, but a natural aspect of the way of life which had formed them over the centuries.

By 1881 the last Indian bands were confined to reservations, which continued to diminish in size with every treaty signed and every treaty broken. The Indians fought back briefly through their religion, most notably through the 'Ghost Dance'. This was conceived in 1889 by a Paiute shaman named Wovoka, during a fever, and spread rapidly through the Plains tribes. It promised the appearance of a Messiah, together with the return of the buffalo and the Indian dead, to herald an Indian resurgence. Wovoka advocated peaceful, innocent behaviour as opposed to an armed uprising. Adherents to the new faith, men and women, also performed the Ghost Dance itself; the main ritual was a circular, shuffling dance, the participants increasing their speed as they sang until they fell into a trance, attaining visions of lost relatives and of the return of past splendour. Visions also revealed sacred designs which were used to embellish Ghost Dance shirts—which in the case of the Sioux tainted the original peaceful faith since they were provocatively proclaimed to make the wearer impervious to bullets.

The glimmer of hope that the Ghost Dance offered was consequently extinguished in late December 1890 when the white authorities, increasingly nervous at the prophecies of the religion, the warlike nature of protective shirts, and the frenzied support the cult had aroused, sent troops to intercept Big Foot's Miniconjou Sioux band who were travelling to collect rations. The band were taken to and surrounded at Wounded Knee Creek; and there, after the start of a Ghost Dance and the firing of a concealed gun by an Indian, Big Foot and a large number of his band were massacred, including many women and children. Conflicting figures have been given by various respected writers, ranging from 128 Indian dead to as many as several hundred, and thus reflecting the problems of accurately chronicling the Plains Indians. Records show that the known dead totalled 153, but to this can be added a number who died subsequently out of the authorities' care, possibly raising the true figure to nearer 180.

The Wounded Knee massacre symbolised the final destruction of the Plains Indians, through the breaking of their spirit.

The Plates

The exact dating of many of these costumes is impossible. Apart from certain general trends, such as the increased use of trade cloth in place of skins as the 19th century progressed, the same costumes were used over a long period.

A: Warriors of 1800–1850

Pictorial information as to the appearance of the Plains Indians before the invention of photography

The Cheyenne sub-chief Yellow Bear, a magnificent example of Cheyenne facial features. (Robin May collection)

is relatively scarce. What knowledge we have is due to artists such as Bodmer and Catlin, who took on the task of portraying the American Indian during the 1830s. We have relied heavily upon their work in illustrating this earlier period, supported by written descriptions and such few artefacts as survive. It is obvious that the garments were far less tailored than they subsequently became, being made of nearly complete skins of deer and sheep.

A1: Hidatsa 'Dog-Soldier' (warrior society member)

Under attack by two Assiniboin warriors, this Hidatsa has staked his long sash-end to the ground, symbolising his vow not to retreat before the enemy unless released by a fellow warrior. He also wears an elaborate feathered headdress, painted and quilled leggings, and quilled moccasins from which hang animal tails. A scalp hangs from his Missouri war hatchet, and he is also armed with a bow and arrows.

A2: Assiniboin warrior

His bow-lance, later to become a ceremonial object, is here used in earnest as a weapon. From his shoulders hangs a buffalo robe. He carries a painted shield complete with attached medicine bundle. It is worth noting that at this period shields were larger than they subsequently became with the development of horseback fighting.

Two Moon(s), a famous Northern Cheyenne warrior; born in 1842 or 1847, he lived until 1917, and is here photographed in a magnificent 'trailer' war bonnet at Ft Keogh in 1878. One of nine Northern Kit Fox 'little chiefs', Two Moon played a prominent part at the Little Bighorn in 1876. In 1913, while visiting Washington, he claimed to have led all the Cheyenne who fought at the Greasy Grass, but Black Wolf dismissed him as 'the biggest liar in the whole Cheyenne tribe'. To this Two Moon retorted that he did not think it wrong to lie to white people! After leading the last band of Cheyenne into Ft Keogh in April 1877, Two Moon became an influential figure; he scouted against the Nez Percé and the Sioux under Col. Nelson 'Bear Coat' Miles, and the whites regarded him as the Chief of the Northern Cheyenne. In fact his own people continued to recognise their own band chiefs, not acknowledging Two Moon as an 'old man chief' until his later years. (National Park Service, US Dept. of the Interior, courtesy Robin May)

A3: Assiniboin warrior
Armed with a typical 'gun-stock' club, he wears a headdress of small feathers and horns, and a typical war shirt and leggings of this early period, decorated with quillwork and paint.

B: The Blackfoot
B1: Member of the Motokiks women's society
In traditional costume, it is impossible to date this figure closely; early skin garments were retained for these purposes after trade cloth had begun to predominate in everyday clothing. Society membership is marked by the so-called 'scabby bull' headdress. The skin dress is decorated with elk teeth, and held at the waist by a long 'tack' belt—i.e. a leather belt decorated with brass tacks. Beaded leggings and moccasins complete the costume. She holds a pipe bag.

B2: Blood warrior
This member of the Blood sub-group of the tribe decorates his hair with strips of ermine. His war medicine hangs from his left shoulder: a bandolier of large seeds, and a bunch of owl and hawk feathers. He wears a cloth shirt with beaded strips—both indicating a mid-19th century date, perhaps—a breechclout, and moccasins. He carries an English-made flintlock musket decorated by him with brass tacks, as is the whip/war club hanging from his right wrist. A 'strike-a-light' (flint-and-steel) hangs from his gun. His shield is hung on his left hip. The end of the long tack belt hangs almost to the ground.

B3: Warrior in winter dress, *second half of the 19th century*
His fur hat is decorated with a solitary eagle feather. The capote or hooded blanket coat, introduced originally by French trappers in the north-east, is made from a striped Hudson's Bay trade blanket. On a leather shoulder strap hang a horn container of some kind—not a powder horn, since he carries a breech-loader—and a spyglass in a leather case. He carries his rifle in a beaded gun case, and a beaded knife sheath is attached to his tack belt. The leggings are also of blanket cloth.

B4: Elder
The ornate bonnet is of the type known as a 'straight up' headdress; it is made of eagle feathers decorated with strips of quillwork, tipped with ermine and horse hair; a cap of ermine, and ermine pendants; and a brow band decorated with brass tacks. The weasel tail shirt—so-called for obvious reasons—is decorated with beaded strip, and over it hangs a bead-wrapped loop necklace. Wrapped around his body and over his left shoulder he wears a blanket decorated with a beaded blanket strip hung with ermine pendants. Floral beaded moccasins complete the costume. In his right hand he carries a pipe and a pipe bag decorated with quill- and beadwork; in his left, a horse stick—an item of war medicine consisting of a carved stick with a horse's head, leather ears, a scalp of black horse hair, coloured buffalo wool and horse tail, adorned with two arrows with leather heads.

C: Three generations of the Blackfoot
C1: Blackfoot mother with child in cradleboard
She wears an old-style buckskin dress decorated with beads and elk teeth. A broad leather tack belt can just be seen at the waist. The cradleboard, traditionally made from curved and cross-braced willow wands, was later replaced by a board sawn to this shape. It is covered with buckskin decorated with floral beadwork, as is the apron which covers the lacing holding the baby. The carrying strap passes round the mother's shoulders and chest; it also allowed the cradleboard to be hung from a saddle pommel or a convenient tree.

C2: Grandmother
She wears a trade cloth headscarf, a sateen trade cloth dress decorated with beads and cowrie shells, shell earrings and many necklaces. She smokes a woman's pipe, and at her feet are her smoking accessories: a cutting board, twist of tobacco, knife, tamping sticks, and a steel for fire-making (also used for sharpening knives).

C3: Minipoka
Loosely translated, a 'favourite', recognisable by the exact replica of an adult female costume which has been lovingly made for her. The blanket dress is decorated with cowrie shells and ribbon; her leggings and moccasins are decorated with beadwork. The doll that she carries is another near-perfect replica of adult costume, down to the detail of a 'strike-a-light' hanging from its belt.

C4: Minipoka
Another lovingly-detailed costume for a special child. He has a split-horn bonnet decorated with weasel strips, ribbons, bells and eagle feathers; a beaded and painted skin shirt; a breechclout, blanket leggings and moccasins, all decorated with typical Blackfoot beadwork. In his left hand is a doll; in his right, a hoop-and-stick game, designed to develop marksmanship—the idea was to throw the feathered stick through the rolling hoop.

D: Fight between Sioux and Crow warriors, mid- to late 19th century
D1: Sioux, Tokala or Kit Fox Society
The society costume consisted of a fox pelt and tail, worn here as a headdress although it could also be

Wolf Robe, a Southern Cheyenne born c.1841, and here photographed in 1909. (Smithsonian Institution, courtesy Robin May)

worn as a sash or belt. Another symbol was the unstrung bow-lance, decorated with beadwork and hung with a loose-flowing cluster of feathers ending in two eagle feathers. He also carries a painted shield and a beaded bowcase and quiver.

On his chest is a 'hair-pipe' breast plate. In the earliest days these thin tubes were made from the central column of the conch shell. By the 17th century white traders were already supplying brass replicas, and silver examples appeared in the 18th century. These metal tubes were unpopular, and before the end of the century traders were supplying shell tubes from New Jersey. Used individually as hair ornaments (thus 'hair-pipes'), they reached the Plains early in the 1800s, and spread as far as the Cheyenne. They were also grouped in large numbers as necklaces, and finally as breast plates. White-manufactured bone hair-pipes were popular for breast plates in the second half of the century.

A breechclout, old-style beaded skin leggings and beaded moccasins complete his costume. His horse blanket is decorated with both quillwork and beadwork.

D2: Sioux, Cante Tinza or Braveheart Society
The society is recognised by the headdress, the feathered lance, and the sabre (captured or traded) with a hanging black otter skin, which was carried by some officers of the society. The headdress is made from split buffalo horns, with ermine

American Horse, a 'Shirt-Wearer' of the Oglala Sioux; the photograph has been captioned elsewhere as having been taken during a delegation to Washington in 1877, but American Horse was already dead by that date. He was fatally wounded in the stomach on 9 September 1876 by soldiers from Gen. George Crook's command, who destroyed his winter camp and appropriated dried buffalo meat for much-needed rations. Note his finely beaded scalp shirt. (Smithsonian Institution, courtesy Robin May)

decorations, a beaded brow band, and a cloth trailer with four lines of eagle feathers. The beaded war shirt is decorated with paint, and horse and human hair. Beaded moccasins are worn with blanket leggings.

D3: Sioux, Kangi Yuha or Crow Owner Society
The marks of the society are the stuffed crow hung round his neck, the black body paint, and the decorations of feathers, otter skin wrap and stuffed crow upon his lance. Another identifying sign is the fact that the undersides of the war shirt sleeves have not been sewn but are only thonged together, allowing him to throw them back for greater freedom of movement in combat. His painted shield hangs from his horse. He is armed with a Colt single-action .45 revolver.

D4: Sioux, Miwatani Society
Also known as the Tall Ones and the Owl Feather Headdress Order, this society wore headdresses of owl feathers surrounding four upright eagle feathers; whistles made from eagle wing bones; and quirts with straps and trailers of otter skin. They, too, wore a 'stake-down' sash. In his right hand is a coup stick, in his left a bow; the society fletched its arrows with owl feathers. He also wears a breechclout and beaded moccasins.

D5: Sioux, Wiciska or White Marked Society
The headdress consists of split horns and an eagle feather trailer; another mark of membership is the hooked lance. In his left hand he carries a club. He wears a bird claw necklace, a quilled breast plate, a quilled knife case, and beaded moccasins, and the painted shield is embellished with bells and feathers.

D6: Crow warrior
Armed with a typical lance, he wears an eagle skin on his head; a shirt decorated with typical Crow beadwork and ermine; quilled and painted leggings, and quilled moccasins. His painted shield is heavily decorated with feathers hung from a lower apron.

D7: Crow warrior
The magnificent headdress of a bear's head and skin and eagle feathers is worn with typical Crow necklaces, a trade cloth breechclout, old-style beaded leggings, and moccasins. The painted shield is decorated with feathers, and the Winchester carbine with brass tacks.
(This plate is based upon the pictographs of Amos Bad Heart Bull, an Oglala Sioux from the Pine Ridge Reservation.)

E: The Arapaho
E1: White Woman
The White Woman was the key figure in the ceremonies of the Arapaho women's Buffalo Society in the earlier part of the 19th century. Her regalia consists of a headdress of swan and goose feathers and down, white weasel skins and buffalo horns; and a wide belt beaded with crosses and bars, hung with buffalo tails, white feathers, and the skins of whip-poor-will and poor-will birds. Her ceremonial dress is decorated with painted symbols and beadwork, and her leggings and moccasins are typical of the fine craftsmanship of the Arapaho.

She holds a whistle in her mouth, and carries two wooden poles which were used to imitate the pounding of buffalo hooves during the ceremony.

E2: Ghost Dancer, 1890

In contrast to the figure of White Woman, representing the early Plains rituals, this illustration shows a participant in the Ghost Dance—the religion of desperation which spread from the Paiutes of Nevada right across the Plains in 1889–90. He is presenting a ceremonial pipe to the Sun, Earth, Fire, and Four Winds prior to passing it to the other dancers. He wears as little as possible to connect him with the white man—e.g. metal. Many Ghost Dancers went so far as to avoid beadwork (since trade beads had a white connotation) or even cloth; but due to the times he lives in this dancer is forced to wear a cloth breechclout, and retains his moccasins. The painted symbols on his Ghost Dance shirt and leggings have a ceremonial significance.

F: The Kiowa and Comanche

Leaving the Rocky Mountains area and travelling south at some time during the early 18th century, these tribes eventually reached the southern Plains. Both were renowned for their adventurous spirit, and the Comanche, in particular, for their horsemanship.

F1: Kiowa brave

Resplendent in a decorated fur turban, he wears a typical southern Plains hide shirt, far more tailored than those favoured by more northerly tribes. His braids are wrapped in elaborate otter skin drops. On his chest is a bone hair-pipe breast plate, from which hangs a pectoral of German silver. Across his lap are his bow case and quiver of mountain lion skin and beadwork. The decorative tabs of his leggings can be seen hanging from beneath the blanket wrapped round his waist. Behind him is his shield, complete with a large bell. In his left hand he carries a medicine arrow-lance, more a ceremonial object than a serious weapon.

F2: Kiowa woman

It is worth comparing the style of her dress with those of the more northerly tribes on earlier plates. The dress has an elaborately cut yoke, but little

Red Cloud, 1822–1909—the renowned leader of the Oglala Sioux, who proved as effective an enemy of the white man through diplomacy as through war. In the mid-1860s he advised the US Army: 'If you want peace, return at once to the Powder River'. When the warning was ignored he completely disrupted the Bozeman Trail from 1866 to 1868; commanded the famous massacre of Capt. Fetterman's 80 men; and forced the whites to reach a settlement on his terms. It was only after the troops had been withdrawn and the forts burned down that Red Cloud added his signature to the Treaty of Ft. Laramie, and retired from the warpath to a spacious reservation. Although he was criticised by the Sioux who remained hostile, he continued to be the most powerful Oglala chief. He obstructed the whites through intelligent diplomacy, securing agencies on the White River in 1873, making military supervision impractical, and, in 1875, demanding an impossible $600 million for the sale of the revered Black Hills of Dakota.

beadwork. It is made from three deerskins, one each for the front and back of the skirt and the third for the bodice. At the waist is a belt decorated with large German silver discs, from which hangs a beautifully beaded flint-and-steel pouch. The typical Kiowa leg-moccasins are decorated with metal bosses and delicate beadwork. Her child peeps out from the safety of a superbly decorated cradle.

F3: Comanche brave

Many Plains Indians were photographed wearing

various headgear obtained from the whites. This is an old 'Jeff Davis' or 'Hardee' military hat, last used in any numbers by the US Army just before the Civil War, during which it was seen in quantity only in Gen. Gibbons' famous 'Iron Brigade' from Wisconsin, Indiana and Michigan. Beneath his blanket this Comanche wears another southern Plains shirt, fringed and decorated with feathers. His hair dressing, chest ornament, long breech-clout, heavily fringed leggings and moccasins are all typical of Comanche costume. He carries a fan of feathers and beadwork, and a spontoon-bladed tomahawk.

F4: Comanche girl
Again, the very limited use of beadwork is typical of the southern Plains tribes. The simplicity of her dress is made up for by the beauty and complexity of her boots of leather and rawhide, decorated with beads and German silver buttons, and painted green with a pigment extracted from pond algae.

G: Battle of the Little Bighorn, 25 June 1876
G1: Cheyenne brave
The Troops of the 7th Cavalry wiped out with Custer were C, E, F, I and L; their guidons were lost, though one was recovered 11 weeks later at Slim Buttes. This brave has seized the guidon of Troop L (identified by the letter in the centre of the ring of stars), and is about to use it as a more than adequate coup stick.

His war bonnet, quirt, saddle blanket, knife case and moccasins are based upon examples in the Haffenreffer Museum of Anthropology. Moccasins, knife case, saddle blanket, and the brow band of the bonnet are all good examples of typical mid-century Cheyenne beadwork: 'lazy stitch' on rawhide. The quirt is attached to his right wrist in the same way as that of G3; its heavy handle makes it a useful club.

According to Cheyenne sources, 12 warriors who fought at the Little Bighorn ('Greasy Grass') wore war bonnets, and ten of these were the type with trailers. As explained in the body of our text, the bonnet did not necessarily denote a chief, as is often supposed; but that the warrior had earned, and claimed, the right and honour of wearing it as a leading brave. The costume is completed by metal arm bands and a trade cloth breechclout. His paint is personal to the warrior. He has also painted his

Chief Gall, the famous Hunkpapa Sioux warrior who led the group which finally cut off from all hope of escape Custer's command of the US 7th Cavalry at the Little Bighorn on 25 June 1876.

horse: lightning marks on the neck, to encourage speed; spots, to represent hail; and a hand mark, indicating an enemy slain in hand-to-hand combat.

G2: Buffalo Calf Road Woman
At the battle of the Rosebud on 17 June 1876, when Gen. Crook's command was severely handled by Crazy Horse, Buffalo Calf Road Woman rescued her brother, Chief Comes-In-Sight. Eight days later this same Cheyenne woman warrior, the wife of Black Coyote, is thought to have fought on horseback at the Greasy Grass. She wears a fine trade cloth dress edged with ribbon and decorated with as many as 300 elk milk-teeth, gathered at the waist by a broad tack belt. Long dentalium earrings, a hair-pipe choker of bone, a trade blanket round the waist and beaded boots complete her costume. The tasselled pommel of her woman's saddle can just be seen, covered by a trade blanket. The bridle is decorated with German silver—as was the harness of many Cheyenne horses, even those of the humblest warriors. She carries a .44 Dragoon Colt. On her cheeks are painted two red circles, representing the rising and setting sun.

G3: Crow scout, US 7th Cavalry

There were six Crow scouts with Custer's force; most of them were probably with Maj. Reno's party at the time of the massacre. Our man wears traditional Crow costume apart from the Army four-button 'sack coat': Custer's scouts were photographed in these coats three years previously. (Full uniform for scouts did not appear until some years after the 1876 war.) His hairstyle is typically Crow: the back is dressed with gum balls, the sides are braided, and the front is swept upwards. From his belt hangs a painted knife case. He wears typical Crow panelled leggings, with a trade cloth breechclout and moccasins. His quirt has a beaded wrist band and an engraved elk antler handle. He is armed with a Springfield carbine.

While the stepped design on these leggings is typical of the Blackfoot, this beadwork pattern was also used by the Sioux, and the fringing suggests that these are, in fact, of Sioux origin.

Bibliography

American Indian Art Magazine

Bancroft-Hunt, *The Indians of the Great Plains* (Orbis)

Blish, *A pictographic History of the Oglala Sioux* (Nebraska)

Burt, *Plains Indians* (Museum of Mankind)

Calf Robe & Hungry Wolf, *Siksika' A Blackfoot Legacy* (Good Medicine)

Conn, *Circles of the World* (Denver Art Museum)

Conn, *Native American Art* (Denver Art Museum)

Conn, *Robes of White Shell and Sunrise* (Denver Art Museum)

Drysdale & Brown, *The Gift of the Sacred Pipe* (Oklahoma)

Ewers, *The Blackfoot: Raiders on the North-Western Plains* (Oklahoma)

Hail, *Hau, Kola* (Haffenreffer Museum of Anthropology)

Hanson, *Metal Weapons, Tools, and Ornaments of the Teton Dakota Indians* (Nebraska)

Hassrick, *The Sioux* (Oklahoma)

Hoebel, *The Cheyennes: Indians of the Great Plains* (Holt, Rinehart & Winston)

Hungry Wolf, *The Blood People* (Harper & Row)

Koch, *Dress Clothing of the Plains Indians* (Oklahoma)

Kroeber, *The Arapaho* (Bison)

Laubin, *Indian Dances of North America* (Oklahoma)

Lowie, *Indians of the Plains* (Bison)

Lowie, *The Crow Indians* (Bison)

Lyford, *Quill and Beadwork of the Western Sioux* (Johnson)

McCracken, *George Catlin and the Old Frontier* (Bonanza)

Mails, *Mystic Warriors of the Plains* (Doubleday)

Marquis, *Wooden Leg* (Bison)

Mayhall, *The Kiowas* (Oklahoma)

Peterson, *Plains Indian Art from Fort Marion* (Univ. of Oklahoma Press)

Powell, *People of the Sacred Mountain* (Harper & Row)

Scherer, *Indians* (Bonanza)

Schmitt and Brown, *Fighting Indians of the West* (Charles Scribner's Sons)

Swanton, *The Indian Tribes of North America* (Smithsonian)

Taylor, *The Warriors of the Plains* (Hamlyn)

The Old West: The Great Chiefs (Time Life)

The Old West: The Indians (Time Life)

The World of the American Indian (National Geographic)

Thomas & Ronnefeldt, *Le Peuple du Premier Homme* (Flammarian)

Thompson, *North American Indian Collection: A Catalogue* (Berne Historical Museum)

Urwin, *The United States Cavalry* (Blandford)

Utley, *The Last Days of the Sioux Nation* (Yale)

Wallace & Hoebel, *The Comanches* (Univ. of Oklahoma Press)

Weist, *History of the Cheyenne People* (Montana)

Wildschut & Ewers, *Crow Indian Beadwork* (Museum of the American Indian Heye Foundation)

Wissler, *North American Indians of the Plains* (American Museum of Natural History)

With Eagle Glance (Museum of the American Indian)

Introduction

The origin of the name 'Apache' is unclear, though it probably stems from the Zuni '*ápachu*', their name for the Navajo, who the early Spaniards called 'Apaches de Nabaju'. One suggested alternative is that it originated in the rare Spanish spelling 'apache' of 'mapache', meaning raccoon, which in view of the distinctive white stripes typically daubed across a warrior's face is rather attractive, if unlikely. The Apaches in fact referred to themselves with variants of '*ndé*', simply meaning, in common with many Indian self-designations, 'the people'.

The Apache culture of 1850 was a blend of influences from the peoples of the Great Plains, Great Basin and the South-West, particularly the Pueblos, and—as time progressed—from the Spanish and American settlers. Tribal peculiarities depended upon geographical location in relation to these peoples, and the time and route of a tribe's early migration. In a work of this size, generalisations concerning 'typical' Apache traits of the Chiricahua, Mescalero, Jicarilla, Western and Lipan Apaches—e.g. the eating of mescal, hunting and gathering economy, the puberty rite, masked impersonators of the Mountain Spirit supernaturals—inevitably have to be made. Tribal and indeed individual divergences naturally occurred in what was a highly individualistic society; but where a reference is made to a *common* trait, it describes a feature considered integral to the rich and distinctive Apachean culture.

An 1880s studio shot of Nalté, a San Carlos Apache warrior, labelled the 'San Carlos dude'. Note the identification tag hanging from his necklace, and the quirt on a thong around his wrist. The Frank Wesson carbine he is holding is a studio prop. (Arizona State Museum, University of Arizona)

The Apache Tribes

The Apachean or Southern Athapaskan language, and therefore the Apache people themselves, can be divided into seven tribal groups: Navajo, Western, Chiricahua, Mescalero, Jicarilla, Lipan, and Kiowa-Apache. For the purposes of this work, the **Navajo**, because they came to be considered as a distinct entity by virtue of developments in their culture, must be excluded. (While they are always regarded as a distinct tribe, their Apachean origins are nevertheless reflected in striking similarities to certain Apache traits.)

Of the six true Apache tribes, the **Kiowa-Apache** were the least integrated into Apache society. The earliest known divergence in language, c.AD1300, occurred between the Western and Kiowa-Apache, the latter separating from the other Apache groups before the beginnings of influence from the Pueblos of the South-West. The Kiowa-Apache remained on the north-eastern fringes of the South-West, and had no historic political con-

A shaman's painted buckskin, embellished with designs invoking supernatural power for curing ceremonies. (Arizona State Museum, University of Arizona)

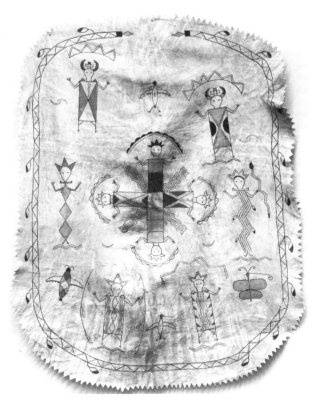

nections with the Apaches. They adopted instead a Plains-orientated culture, closely related, as their name suggests, to the Kiowa Indians. While retaining their own identity the Kiowa-Apache, despite their alien language and origin, formed a component part of the Kiowa camp-circle and society.

The Apache tribes most closely related to the Kiowa-Apache were the **Lipan**, who had a lesser degree of Plains influence in their culture. They had a weakly developed band organisation, reportedly consisting of three bands in the early 19th century. These bands probably corresponded to the Lipanjenne, Lipanes de Arriba and Lipanes Abajo described by Orozco y Berra (1864).

Jicarilla

The closest relations of the Lipan were the Jicarilla Apache, whose mountainous territory ranged from north-eastern New Mexico into southern Colorado. The Jicarilla, whose name comes from the Spanish 'little basket' in reference to the women's expertise in basket-weaving, numbered about 800 in 1850. They were divided into two bands. Those west of the Rio Grande were known as '*saidindé*', 'sand people', and comprised six local groups. They were also known by the Spanish name Olleros, 'potters'—although, as they were a mountain people, it has been suggested that this should be Hoyeros, 'people of the mountain dells'. The eight local groups east of the Rio Grande were the '*gulgahén*' or Llaneros, meaning 'plains people'. They comprised, at least in part, the Plains Apache group referred to as Lipiyanes, whose Cuartalejo, Paloma and Carlena bands were absorbed into the Jicarilla after 1800. While there was no linguistic or cultural division between the eastern and western bands, membership depending simply on residence, there was a strong two-band consciousness. The competitiveness between the moieties, best illustrated by the annual ceremonial relay race, was similar to that of the northern Pueblos of the Rio Grande.

Mescalero

South of the Jicarilla Apache were the Mescalero. The name is a Spanish term meaning 'mescal makers': a reference to their extensive use of the agave or century mescal plant which made an important contribution to Apache subsistence. The Mescalero lived among the Sacramento, Guadalupe and Davis Mountains of south-east New Mexico and western Texas, their homeland centring on the forbidding 12,000-foot peak of Sierra Blanca. Their hunting range spread south into Mexico, and east of the Pecos River on to the Plains. The Mescalero were loosely divided into the '*gulgahénde*', 'people of the Plains', east of the mountains; and the '*ni't'áhende*', 'earth crevice people', living in the mountains. Tribal culture was, however, uniform throughout, and this purely geographical division had no definite boundaries or function. Organisation into bands was weakly developed, most bands being known by the name of the mountain range that they occupied. The main Mescalero band were the Sierra Blanca, while the Apache group known as the Faraones made up a southern division. Band territories were poorly defined, just as they were among the other buffalo-hunting Apache tribes. This was perhaps dictated, in the case of the Mescalero, by the fact that buffalo herds roamed only in the eastern lowlands; so only with a fluid system of weakly defined bands and boundaries could tribesmen from other parts of the Mescalero range share in this vital resource.

Chiricahua

Division into bands was far more important to the Chiricahua, probably the most famous Apache tribe. They were divided into three bands, each with minor cultural differences. A confusing variety of ambiguous names have been used to denote various parts of the Chiricahua, but the band divisions can be simplified as follows.

The Eastern Chiricahua inhabited territory in south-west New Mexico, west of the Rio Grande. Their Chiricahua name was '*čihéne*' meaning 'red paint people', because of the red band typically daubed across their faces. The term Gileños or Gila Apaches was used at different times by the Spaniards to denote various groups. It specifically denoted, however, those Apaches living at the headwaters of the Gila River, and can be treated as synonymous with the Eastern Chiricahua. The Eastern Chiricahua or Gileños were, after 1800, identified as containing two distinct groups: the Mimbres and the Mogollon Apaches, each named after the mountain ranges they inhabited. The

Naiché, son of Cochise of the Central Chiricahua, 1880. He wears a magnificent owl-feather war-cap which invoked supernatural power for swiftness and protection in battle. (Arizona State Museum, University of Arizona)

Mimbres or Mimbreños were also known as Coppermine Apaches, and were at times divided into two closely related groups, known as the Coppermine (Mimbres) Apaches and the Warm Springs (Ojo Caliente) Apaches.

While Geronimo's people, the Bedonkohe Apaches, have sometimes been referred to as a distinct tribe, its seems likely that they were identical with the Mogollon Apaches. Thus, the Eastern Chiricahua band (Gileños) comprised the Mimbreños (Coppermine or Mimbres, and Warm Springs Apaches) and Mogollon (Bedonkohe) Apache groups.

The second Chiricahua band were the Chokonens, also known as the central or true Chiricahua and the Cochise Apaches, after their renowned leader. Their lands stretched into Mexico and New Mexico from south-east Arizona's Chiricahua

White Mountain Apache scouts, with Gen. George Crook in the background in his distinctive white pith helmet. Note the Plains-like shield hung with eagle feathers held by a scout in the foreground. The date is uncertain, being either mid-1870s or mid-1880s. (Arizona State Museum, University of Arizona)

Mountains, which gave the band and the tribe their name, and which contained the infamous Apache Pass.

South of the true Chiricahua were the third and final band, the Southern Chiricahua, who ranged the Sierra Madre region of northern Mexico. They were known as the Nednhi, 'enemy people', and were sometimes referred to, in part or whole, as Pinery or Bronco Apaches.

Western Apache

North of the Chiricahua tribe were the Western Apache of Arizona, who were, in the 1800s, divided into five autonomous groups based on slight differences in dialect.

The easternmost and largest group were the White Mountain Apache, whose lands stretched from the Pinaleño Mountains in the south to the White Mountains in the north. They were divided into the Eastern White Mountain and Western White Mountain bands, and sometimes referred to as Coyoteros. An earlier division into the Sierra Blanca (White Mountain) in the north and Coyotero in the south has been suggested.

To the north of the White Mountain Apache were the Cibecue group, whose lands reached well north of the Mogollon Rim, skirted to the west by the Sierra Ancha. The Cibecue contained the Carrizo, Cibecue and Canyon Creek bands. To the south-west were the San Carlos group, roaming the foothills of the Galuiro and Santa Catalina Mountains. They comprised the San Carlos, Apache Peaks, Pinal and Arivaipa bands, the last two possibly originating in the absorption of distinct Pinaleños and Arivaipa Apaches. Because the language of the San Carlos group was used in early studies, their name is sometimes applied to all the Western Apache.

To the north-west were the Northern and Southern Tonto groups. The Southern Tonto, ranging north from the Sierra Ancha and Mazatzal mountains, were divided into the Mazatzal band and six unnamed semi-bands. The Northern Tonto, who lived just south of the San Francisco mountains, contained the Bald Mountain, Fossil Creek, Mormon Lake and Oak Creek bands. The Tonto groups, particularly the Northern Tonto, were very closely related to the Yuman tribe called the Yavapais. The name Tonto was used to denote the south-eastern Yavapais, and it is thought that the Tonto divisions of the Western Apache may have originated in intermarriage between these Indians and Apaches. While the division of the Tonto Apaches into northern and southern groups is an integral part of Goodwin's authoritative interpretation of Western Apache society, the Tontos always regarded themselves as a single group.

Various names have been applied to all or parts of the Western Apache. They have been referred to collectively as Tontos, though this term in its widest sense was usually applied to those Yuman and Apache groups occupying the Tonto Basin. The term 'Pinaleños' has been used as a major division of the Western Apache, but usually refers to those Indians roaming the Pinal Mountains. Both the entire Western Apache tribe and the White Mountain division have been described as Coyoteros.

The Apache tribes can be divided into three groups according to language, and to the time of migration into the historic area. The Western Apache, Mescalero and Chiricahua form what can be described as the typical Apache group, to which the Navajo originally belonged. The second group comprises the Jicarilla and Lipan, and the third the Kiowa-Apache. Cultural distinctions among the Apache conform with these divisions to a certain degree, those tribes living in close contact with each other sharing certain traits. Thus there were close

links between the Chiricahua and Mescalero, who were the last tribes to assume separate identities.

The geographical position of the tribes similarly affected their culture, through the influence of non-Apachean tribes and contact with the people of the South-West, Plains and Great Basin. Where generalisations are made about the Apache tribes as a whole, the Kiowa-Apache, by virtue of their strong affiliation with the Plains, tend to deviate severely from the norm, and should not be considered.

Apache Life

Social Structure

The social structure of the Apache people followed a typical pattern. The Apache population was thinly spread, scattered into relatively small groups across large tribal territories. Such an existence in a harsh environment did not lend itself to a regimented social structure. Consequently, tribal cohesion was minimal, without central leadership, and consisted basically of recognition of a distinct culture, and hospitality towards those of like customs, language and dress. Similarly, members of a particular Apache band had a degree of internal unity, claiming certain hunting grounds, recognising one another's distinctive dialect, and acknowledging the band into which they were born throughout their life. Central leadership and joint political action were, however, very limited and rarely seen.

The largest practical unit was the local group, the nucleus of government, social organisation, hunting, warfare and the practice of religious ceremonies. The hostile environment which prevented a closely knit society at tribal level, conversely encouraged the gregarious nature and cohesion of the Apache people within the local group. This was further enhanced by the close relationships between most members of the local group, either by blood or marriage. They gathered together, around an elder who acted as spokesman, and by whose name the group might be known.

A beautiful example of an Apache war-charm necklace of shell and stone tied into entwined leather thongs, hung with eagle 'fluffies' and feathers. (Arizona State Museum, University of Arizona: photo Helga Teiwes)

Local group leadership was the most extensive example of Apache government and was the position that tribal chiefs such as Cochise and Victorio held. The local group leader was expected to display courage in war, generosity towards the needy, and eloquence in speaking at public occasions. He was also expected to demonstrate an affinity with the Apache's sacred powers, through the knowledge and authority to perform certain religious ceremonies. Like the Plains Indian chiefs, an Apache leader did not dictate to his people, but exerted his influence upon them, promoting decisions he believed to be for the common good. His rôle was to maintain harmony through consultation with other family heads, and to arbitrate in disputes among the Apaches, who had a

An Apache 'flop-head' war-club, clearly showing the rawhide encasement, and a superb horse-hair trailer. (Arizona State Museum, University of Arizona: photo Helen Teiwes)

keen sense of family honour. A popular spokesman who proved to be a good provider would lead a thriving local group, while a declining leader would be gently displaced as another man's voice gained more weight in council. An inadequate man rarely rose to prominence, for the Apaches knew their men too well. While the local group leader's rôle was not hereditary, a leader's son often inherited the status simply through the influence and education which he had gained from his father.

The local group comprised up to 30 extended families. These ideally consisted of a man and wife, unmarried sons and daughters, and married daughters with their husbands and children, gathered into a family cluster, each nuclear family occupying a separate dwelling. The local group was associated with a particular settlement, and often known by the name of a nearby landmark such as a river or forest. The settlement, a place of superior defence, shelter, and food, water and grazing resources, provided a focal point for the local group. Family headmen met there to discuss the exploitation of the surrounding resources. The actual execution of most economic tasks was carried out by the extended family, who were reasonably self-sufficient within the local group's confines. They would leave the settlement to hunt or gather food, and return to process it.

The Apache women provided the constant thread through generations of an extended family, since after marriage it was customary for a man to join his wife's relatives. While marriage often took place between unrelated members of the same local group, if a man did marry into an outside group he had to make the transition to life in another territory.

Women were eligible for marriage after puberty, men after they had accepted adult responsibilities as warriors and hunters, usually in their early twenties. The marriage ceremony was simple, usually involving an exchange of gifts (as in the case of the Plains Indians), which might persist between the intermarried families for several years. The construction of a new shelter for the married couple, within the girl's family cluster, confirmed the marriage. The newly married man showed respect for his new relatives through avoidance practices and the use of polite forms of speech. He was obliged to work for his wife's parents, who called him 'he who carries burdens for me'. While the Apache was fiercely individual, he was also taught from an early age to put the good of his extended family first. A conscientious husband could, after becoming the head of his own family, aspire to leadership of the extended family, and eventually of the local group.

While polygamy was reported in all Apache tribes except the Lipan, it was not a common practice. Only a wealthy man might marry twice, and usually to the sister of his first wife.

The division of the Apache tribal groups into bands, local groups and extended families was further complicated in the case of the Western Apache by the existence of a matrilineal clan system reminiscent of the Western Pueblo. There were 62 clans, their members claiming descent from mythological women, and the clans taking their names—e.g. 'two rows of yellow spruce coming together people'—from the farm sites these women established. All clans were ultimately descended from one of three mythological clans, so forming phratries. These clans and phratries interwove all the Western Apache groups. Since a clan's members felt obliged to aid each other, they consequently created extensive tribal links, binding together the isolated local groups. A man's clan could apparently be identified through peculiarities in ceremony, mannerisms, dress—merely by the tilt of his headband—and by clan designs embellishing clothing and possessions.

Marriage between members of clans related to each other within the same phratry was prohibited in the Western Apache, just as the other Apache tribes scorned marriage between close kin. Incest was very closely linked in Apache beliefs to evil witchcraft, the practical necessity of preventing such marriages thus being emphasised through the medium of religion.

Hunting and Gathering

'Apacheria', the land of the Apaches, was a rugged, hostile territory of climatic extremes, descending from forested mountain peaks to desert lowlands, with temperatures ranging from August's 100°F to below zero in winter. Through the evolution of generations, the Apaches developed an innate knowledge of, and affinity with, their homeland. Against a daunting backdrop of canyons, mesas and deserts, they hunted, foraged and fought to survive,

just as the woodrat, lizard and rattlesnake survived.

The Apache eked out a contented, if challenging existence by hunting game and foraging for fruits, seeds and roots of wild plants. A limited amount of agriculture was practised, particularly among the Jicarilla, Western Apache and Lipan, who planted and irrigated plots of corn, beans, maize and squash. All the Apache, however, were primarily hunters and gatherers.

The wild game of Apacheria was as varied as the terrain itself. Deer, antelope, elk and bighorn were the principal large prey in the mountains, foothills and flatlands, while the Mescalero, Jicarilla, Lipan and Kiowa-Apache also ventured on to the Plains in search of buffalo. Diet was supplemented by meat from smaller animals such as woodrats, cottontail rabbits and opossums. Added to this was the Spanish bounty of strayed and captured domestic cattle, as well as horses and mules which were eaten

A fine example of a rawhide medicine-shield, decorated with cloth border, paint designs and hawk feathers, and imparting both physical and supernatural protection to the Apache warrior. (Arizona State Museum, University of Arizona: photo Helga Teiwes)

to stave off starvation. Despite the fact that their lands yielded only enough to survive, and no more, some Apache groups rejected the meat of certain animals in accordance with religious taboos. Coyotes, bears, and snakes were commonly feared as carriers of sickness and embodiments of evil spirits. Certain birds, such as the turkey, were not eaten because of their own diet of worms and insects; while fish, because of their slimy, scaly surface, were associated with the snake.

Hunting was the responsibility of the men, who usually worked alone, in pairs, or in small groups. They chased large game on horseback with lance and bow, used masks crafted from animals' heads to approach deer and antelope on foot, and trapped animals in snares. The men sometimes co-operated in mounted relays to run deer to exhaustion, while the local group might provide the numbers required to surround buffalo, antelope or even rabbits. Among the Chiricahua, however, hunting was so male-dominated that even the presence of a basket woven by a woman might be considered unlucky.

Apache boys learnt the art of bow and arrow from their grandfathers, and after making their first small kill were taught the whistles, calls, habits, and religious mystique of all the animals and birds. The mature hunter was as keen, cunning and hardy as the animals he sought, and knew the peculiarities of his hunting grounds instinctively. As one old Apache commented: 'There is food everywhere if one only knows how to find it.' This was paralleled in the religion of the Western Apache, who believed that a hunter was less successful in a neighbouring group's territory because he drew power from the very ground itself when hunting in his own lands.

The gathering of vital wild plant harvests for food, medicines and weaving materials was the women's prerogative. They knew their land as intricately as the men, and camps were regularly relocated as the seasons changed and women frantically sought to harvest the numerous different plants as they ripened. Young girls were taught to rise early, and to be strong and vigorous. They were trained to carry wood and keep a fresh supply of water; to flesh, tan, dye and sew buckskin into clothes, bags and parfleches; to weave baskets, and fashion them into water-carriers with a covering of piñon pitch; to dry and store foods; to supervise the home and children, and to prepare the meals. So, too, were they instructed in the vital lore of harvesting and preparing the wild plants.

The Apaches tended to endure the cold of winter in villages on the desert lowlands where the cold was not so extreme. When spring arrived in March the members of a local group travelled back into the mountains to their main settlement. Here they established their clusters of 'wickiups': domed shelters consisting of cottonwood poles set in a circular trench, bent and lashed together at the top with yucca fibre. Except in times of wind and rain this framework was only partially covered, with a thatch of bear grass tied with yucca fronds and usually with several hides. While the wickiup was

An Apache baby bound into a typical cradleboard of wicker and cloth, with several protective amulets on a large sun-shade, and decoration of a distinctive T-shaped beaded ornament, and beaded drops. Early 1900s. Around it are baskets, pitch-covered water jar, burden basket, bow and arrow and cloth saddlebag. (Arizona State Museum, University of Arizona)

the typical Apache dwelling, being easily constructed and as easily abandoned in flight from an enemy, the tipi was often erected on the flatlands, particularly by those tribes showing most Plains influence.

Digging sticks broke the ground for the planting of crops, perhaps watered by irrigation ditches. The crops were tended by the young and elderly, while there was a constant coming and going of hunting and gathering parties. The women of the extended family formed a stable, experienced gathering unit, often departing to a nearby gathering ground for a day's work. Major expeditions were also organised, consisting of large hunting parties, gathering groups, or a combination of the two, leaving the settlement for weeks at a time.

After the welcome gathering of the first green vegetables, the narrow-leafed yucca, parties of women sought out the yucca flowers, arrowheads, wild onions, cacti fruits and various berries of spring and early summer. The largest expedition took place in May, when the majority of the local group's women, with all the male assistance they could muster, travelled to an area abundant in the new, towering, reddish spike-leaved stalks of the mescal

A traditional Western Apache buckskin blouse decorated with beadwork and tin cone pendants. (Arizona State Museum, University of Arizona: photo Helga Teiwes)

or agave, also known as the century plant. The mescal stalks were cut, pounded and roasted, and the heavy, fleshy tubers or crowns were prised from the ground with hammers and pointed sticks.

The women worked feverishly, gathering great quantities of the two-foot-diameter mescal crowns and loading them into a huge roasting pit hacked out of the hard, dry soil. Hot stones steamed the mescal into a paste, which was eaten immediately or pounded into flat cakes and sun-dried. The dried mescal was carried home by heavily laden horses, strung out in pack trains, accompanied by the singing, chattering women. The mescal was highly nutritious and could be preserved indefinitely, providing an important staple of the Apache diet.

Throughout the summer and autumn plants were gathered: wild potatoes, and a mixture of acorns, hackberries and mesquite beans, made into crude breads; chokecherries and raspberries dried into cakes; sumal and juniper berries, strawberries, grapes and sweet pink yucca fruit; and wild tobacco, which was cut and cured. In the evenings the extended family's women prepared meals from their spoils and meat, often under shades called ramadas or 'squaw-coolers'.

In October the domestic corn was harvested, and eaten, preserved or brewed by the women into a weak corn beer, called 'tiswin' by the whites. Late autumn provided the best hunting, while women and children amassed copious quantities of acorns, piñon nuts and seeds. As winter, the season called Ghost Face, approached, the Apaches sought the shelter of lowland villages. Gathering largely ceased, while raiding, preserved foods, a limited amount of small game, and food taken in emergencies from secret caches in sealed caves fed the Apache until the yucca stalks reannounced the arrival of spring.

The Apaches were supremely dependent upon nature. Tribal variations on the seasonal pattern varied simply with environment, as each band exploited whatever its particular area yielded.

War

A 1911 photograph of an Apache woman carrying her child in a woven burden basket by means of a headstrap. She wears a traditional fringed buckskin blouse decorated with paint, beadwork, tin cone pendants, and brass studs. (Arizona State Museum, University of Arizona)

The Apache drew a sharp distinction between warfare and raiding. Their respective aims were summarised by the Western Apache words for each: raiding was 'to search out enemy property', while war meant 'to take death from an enemy'.

The raid was prompted by the announcement, usually from an older woman, that the meat supply was approaching exhaustion. The local group's leader, or an experienced warrior, would shortly thereafter announce plans for an expedition, and call for followers. Usually a raiding party consisted of less than a dozen raiders, for concealment was a prime consideration. The rituals preceding a raid were designed to prevent the raiders' discovery, rather than to fortify them for war.

In early times the raids were directed against other Indian tribes, such as the Comanches, but latterly the Spanish and Mexicans generously, if unwittingly, supplied horses and other livestock to the clandestine raiders. Having reached enemy territory the Apache raiders proceeded with great stealth, until they located a tribe's herd. Then, in the early hours of morning, two or three men silently coaxed the livestock a safe distance from the

camp, where their fellow raiders encircled them and drove them off. The return journey was made as rapidly as possible, and by travelling without sleep for up to five days the Apache raiders usually made a successful escape. They avoided fighting, for this would alert their enemies for miles around and defeat the purpose of the raid. If they were pursued and caught the raiders preferred to kill the captured animals, scatter, and return later to devour their spoils.

Upon returning to camp the raiders distributed the livestock among their relatives. They were also obliged to present a proportion of their spoils to widows and divorcées, whose request was embodied in singing and dancing. This ensured an even distribution of meat throughout the local group.

War parties were organised to avenge the deaths of Apache raiders, or Apache families killed by other tribes' raiding parties. The deceased's relatives initiated the organisation of the war party. They called for warriors—particularly kinsmen of the slain Apache—from other local groups to meet at an arranged rendezvous. Here a war ceremony was conducted, called 'stiff hide spread on the ground' by the Western Apache. A shaman versed in the supernatural songs and ceremonials of war conducted prayers exhorting success for, and blood lust in, the warriors, who sang softly and joined the dancing to signify their participation in the war party.

War parties might contain as many as 200 men. Among them would be at least one shaman, who conducted prayers exhorting success for, and blood the venture before they departed. He continued to conduct his ceremonies on the warpath, while also encouraging respectful behaviour from the warriors, for war was a religious undertaking. Having ensured the safety of their local group camps, who might scatter and reunite at a new campsite to avoid back-tracking, the war party departed. They travelled warily, posting scouts when they camped (usually on the highest possible terrain, no matter how far from water and wood), until they reached their target. They often made their attack from several directions at once.

The Apaches preferred to make a surprise attack shortly before dawn. Only the Lipan and the Kiowa-Apache counted coup, the other Apaches extracting revenge by killing as many of the enemy as possible. Scalping was rare, and was probably only practised against the Mexicans in retaliation for their own outrages. (The taking of scalps was not consistent with Apache fears of contamination from the dead, and if practised by a Jicarilla, for example, it required lengthy ritual preparation and subsequent purification.) A single significant victory was usually sufficient to persuade the warriors to return home, particularly if they had acquired livestock and other booty. They were welcomed with celebratory feasting and dancing.

The Apaches were trained for war from boyhood. Boys woke early and bathed in the river, even if they had to crack the surface ice to do so. They ran up hillsides and back with a mouthful of water, to learn correct breathing through the nose, and the endurance so characteristic of the Apaches. Boys were hardened by rough wrestling games and mock battles, and taught by their relatives the geography, attributes and sanctity of their surroundings.

When he felt ready, an Apache youth began the novice warrior complex of his first four raids, which were permeated with religious beliefs and ritual. Having been accepted as a member of his first

raiding party the adolescent was usually instructed by a war shaman, who gave him a drinking tube and scratcher embellished with lightning designs, and a special war cap which, unlike those of the mature warriors, did not bestow spiritual 'power'. Among the Western Apache the men and women of the camp formed a line, and blessed the boy with pollen as he departed.

A White Mountain Apache male doll of cloth, buckskin, feathers, beads and horsehair. (Arizona State Museum, University of Arizona: photo Helga Teiwes)

During the expedition the apprentice warrior was considered sacred, being identified with the culture-hero called Child of the Water. He was obliged to use the ceremonial warpath language, using ritual phrases to replace words for common objects during the raid. He used the scratcher to scratch himself and the drinking tube to ensure water did not touch his lips. The boy also observed such taboos as only eating food after it had grown cold, to bring the raiders good fortune.

The novice's practical rôle was subservient to the other warriors. He fetched wood and water, cooked the food, and guarded the camp at night. If he followed his instructions well, he would be allowed to accompany the warriors on a subsequent raid. If he completed the sacred number of four raids without deviations in his conduct, the novice received the coveted reward of recognition as an Apache warrior.

The legendary skill and endurance of the Apache warriors is supported by the testimonies of the white soldiers who fought them. The 'tigers of the human race', as Gen. George Crook described the Apaches, were ideally adapted to fighting in their rugged homeland. A warrior usually wore a shirt, a breechclout, and moccasins, often reaching above the knee; he carried a rope, blanket, water jar, fire drill, rations of mescal or jerky, and his weapons. He might employ a shield, bow and arrows, lance, war club, knife and, particularly during the Apache Wars, a gun and cartridge belts. The Apaches often blackened their weapons for camouflage (which explains the Mexican name for Warm Springs leader Cuchillo Negro, 'Black Knife').

An Apache could live instinctively off the land, and when nature was ungenerous he could withstand extraordinary extremes of thirst and hunger. A warrior's only other requirements were the amulets prepared by a shaman possessing the ceremonials of war. Buckskin cords and strings worn around the head and over the shoulder; war shirts; medicine shields; tight-fitting war caps adorned with owl and turkey feathers, and numerous other ornaments were embellished with designs invoking the protection and potency of the sacred powers and their bird and animal messengers. Paint was daubed across the warrior's face to invoke the particular power of a war shaman, and bags of sacred cattail pollen or '*hoddentin*' were carried to make morning and evening offerings.

The possession of supernatural 'enemies-against' power was a prized gift, and could be gained either from communion with the sacred powers or directly from a war shaman who had so acquired it. The ceremonials invoking such power might be directed toward protecting a warrior, concealing a war

White Mountain Apache infant's moccasins, decorated with tin cone pendants. (Arizona State Museum, University of Arizona: photo Helga Teiwes)

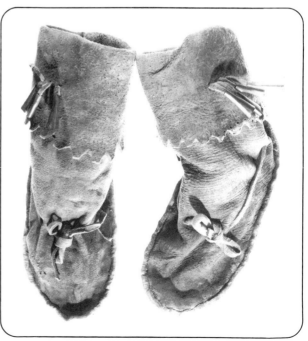

Traditional Western Apache beaded moccasins, with buckskin uppers and rawhide soles. (Arizona State Museum, University of Arizona: photo Helga Teiwes)

party, bestowing speed of running, or locating an enemy. Geronimo was a war shaman whose power allegedly enabled him to predict events, and prevented his being killed by bullets. Victorio's sister, Lozen, who was a woman warrior—a rare thing indeed—had great power: stretching out her arms and praying, she was supposed to be able to determine the proximity of an enemy by the intensity of the tingling in her palms.

While the Apache did adopt a horse culture based on that of the Spaniards, their terrain and lifestyle did not lend itself to the adoption of the horse in the same way as did that of the Plains Indians. Horses were often used during large raids, but a warrior was equally likely to travel on foot, allowing him to use the concealment offered by his terrain. The broad-chested, sinewy Apache warrior could run as much as 70 miles a day, and his 'smooth, effortless stride' was such that, to Lt. Britton Davis, 'the thought of attempting to catch one of them in the mountains gave me a queer feeling of helplessness'. The women were also extraordinary runners, and thought nothing of trotting 60 miles to present candy to their children when they had been placed in boarding schools in later years.

The Apache's adeptness at concealment was demonstrated to Capt. John C. Cremony by the Mescalero called Quick Killer. On an open plain, Quick Killer told Cremony to turn his back, and in an instant had disappeared. Failing to find him, Cremony called for Quick Killer to reveal himself, whereupon the much amused Apache emerged from the spot a few feet away where he had completely buried himself under thick grama grass.

The warriors' skills were easily adapted to the guerrilla war they fought against the Spaniards, Mexicans and Americans. Few pursuers successfully found their way into the labyrinthine strongholds of Apacheria until they learned to turn Apache against Apache, harnessing the remarkable tracking abilities of the scouts. If chased closely an Apache group would scatter, running across rocks to an agreed rendezvous, and leaving no trail. Numerous secret supply caches fed the group, who visited at night the waterholes which they knew well or could quickly spot from high ground. If pressed hard they might kill their horses and climb 'like deer' up seemingly impassable cliffsides.

A young Apache woman photographed in 1920. She wears a typical cluster of bead necklaces, and her cape appears to be tied both at the neck and around the waist. (Arizona State Museum, University of Arizona: photo Forman Hanna)

False camps were sometimes pitched, and livestock driven several miles ahead of the actual area where a group concealed themselves. Camps could be moved silently, and were at times moved right under the noses of the Apaches' enemies. Adept at flight, the Apaches were also skilled in doubling back 'like a fox' and ambushing their pursuers.

The Apaches, in contrast to the Plains Indians, applauded courage but derided heroics: their numbers were too few for flamboyant risks and needless loss of life. Stealth and caution were encouraged—though when the Apache was wounded or cornered there was no more ferocious adversary.

Religion

The Apaches had a rich cycle of sacred myths to explain the origins of their ceremonies and religious beliefs. An unclearly defined Supreme Being was referred to as *Usen* or Life Giver; and myths among the Jicarilla, Lipan and Western Apache told of their people's emergence from within the earth. The popular mythological trickster figure of Coyote created daylight through playing a 'moccasin game', pitting creatures of the night against the victorious creatures of the day. Since the contest resulted in daybreak, whenever the Apache played the moccasin game they would blacken their faces if ever it continued beyond sunrise. Coyote exemplified the virtues and failings of man, securing such necessities as fire while simultaneously demonstrating the vices—gluttony, falsehood, incest—of which the Apaches strongly disapproved.

The most prominent Apache supernaturals were the sacred maiden White Painted Woman (White Shell Woman, Changing Woman) and her son Child of the Water. His brother, Killer of Enemies, is also prominent, though at times the two seem synonymous. Myths of the Apache's early existence focus on White Painted Woman's divine conception of her sons, and their slaying of the evil monsters that inhabited the Earth. The mythological exploits of the culture-heroes, and the rituals and objects they employed, were adopted by the Apaches into their ceremonies. The central participants in the girl's puberty rite and the boy's novice raiding complex were identified with White Painted Woman and Child of the Water respectively.

The Apaches believed the Universe to be permeated with supernatural power, which could be sought by man through prayer, or through a long period of isolated instruction from a shaman who possessed power. Those people who were themselves sought out by a power were regarded as particularly worthy and sacred. A power appeared to its recipient through visionary experience in the form of an animal, bird or natural force related to its type. The visionary was often led to a holy home such as a mountain cave, where he received the

Gan or Mountain Spirit dancers, early 1900s, probably Western Apache judging by the elaborate fan-racks. They wear blankets instead of buckskin kilts, and the central figure wears boots rather than moccasins. However, their extensive black and white body paint, and their wands, cloth and eagle feather arm-trailers, bandanas, masks with false button eyes, and racks clearly bearing snake designs, are traditional. Note the sacred clown on the left wearing a mask, small rack, arm-trailers and white, black-speckled paint. They form the old-time *gan* group of four dancers, symbolising the Four Directions, complemented by a clown. (Arizona State Museum, University of Arizona: photo Forman Hanna)

songs, prayers and ceremonies which were part of, and belonged to, the power; and with which it could be manipulated by the visionary.

Under the guidance of an established shaman a visionary learnt the extent of his power, and its accompanying taboos, for the supernatural had to be treated with great respect. Because illness was so catastrophic to people of a hunting and gathering economy, most powers and their rituals were curative; others were used for such purposes as protection on the warpath, and even to attain success in gambling. Female shamans were apparently quite common, while the possession of power was considered vital to a man who aspired to leadership.

Power could also be used for evil, however. The Apache had strong witchcraft fears, believing witches to covertly cause sickness and even death through the misuse of their powers. Those tried and found guilty of witchcraft—in a trial the Western Apache termed 'they are talking about witches'— were at the very least expelled from the local group.

Closely associated with such witchcraft fears was the distress caused by the presence of creatures such as owls, coyotes, bears and snakes. Such evil familiars were believed to contain the ghosts of witches and other restless spirits who had not departed peacefully after death to the Apaches' parallel underworld. On one of Crook's expeditions into the Sierra Madre his Apache scouts suddenly halted, refusing to go any further until the photographer A. Frank Randall released the owl he had caught and tied to his saddle. Shamans who had power over such creatures, and who could cure the sicknesses they caused, were afforded great respect.

The most noted traditional Apache ceremony was the girl's puberty rite. As a child grew up, various rituals were conducted in prayer for a long and healthy life. Amulets were ritually hung on a baby's cradle board to protect the child, who was particularly vulnerable to evil. When able to walk, the child was led in new footwear along a trail of pollen leading east, in the 'putting on moccasins' ceremony. In the haircutting rite the following spring—a time of new growth—the child's hair was cut, with a few tufts left to encourage healthy growth of new hair and, by extension, of the child. At puberty it was hoped that a boy would make his

A striking 1890s portrait of an unidentified Apache scout wearing a breech-clout over a thin leather belt. The holster on his cartridge-belt holds a US Army Colt revolver. (Arizona State Museum, University of Arizona)

first four sacred raids, while a girl performed the puberty rite, also called the Sunrise Dance.

In the four-day puberty rite, the girl was considered sacred, being identified with White Painted Woman. She wore a beautifully decorated dress of the finest buckskin, coloured yellow to symbolise the sacred pollen. She carried a scratching stick and drinking tube, a cane to symbolise longevity, and wore symbols such as eagle feathers, and shell ornaments which represented White Painted Woman. The ceremonies began on the first morning when the girl, her face daubed with pollen, was led to the ceremonial tipi by the specially appointed shaman whose relentless chanting of songs and prayers accompanied the rituals. The girl knelt on a buckskin, her hands raised to the

sun, in the mythological position assumed by White Painted Woman. Then she lay prone and her female sponsor, a woman of exemplary reputation, massaged her, ensuring her strength as an adult. The sponsor then pushed the girl away, and she ran to the four directions, circling a basket laden with ritual objects, and so receiving a blessing of quickness.

In the evening the maiden attended the ritual singing and dancing in the ceremonial tipi, while social dancing took place outside. Then came the appearance of one of the most dramatic features pervading the ceremonies of the Apache tribes: the masked impersonators of the Mountain Spirits who protected the tribes. The 'gan' or Mountain Spirit dancers invoked the power of these supernaturals to cure illness, drive away evil and bring good fortune. They assembled in a cave in the mountains, and under the guidance of a *gan* shaman donned their sacred regalia. As impersonators of the supernatural they manipulated great power, and therefore observed severe restrictions. To don the *gan* mask without correct ritual; to recognise a friend beneath the mask; to dance incorrectly or to tamper with *gan* regalia after it had been ritually abandoned in a secret cache, might cause sickness, madness or death.

At the appropriate moment in the puberty rite the gan dancers descended from their mountain hideaway. They wore buckskin moccasins and skirts, and masks of black buckskin topped with towering, decorated horns of yucca. Their bodies bore striking paint designs of lightning and other sacred symbols, and they were adorned with red flannel and eagle feather streamers, turquoise and abalone.

Emerging from the darkness four times, they danced, stamped and threatened around a blazing fire, brandishing and thrusting great decorated wands. The *gan*— their groups of four each accompanied by the antics of a white, black-spotted

An Apache warrior's buckskin war-medicine cap, adorned with brass tacks, a silver conch, and eagle feathers. (Arizona State Museum, University of Arizona: photo Helga Teiwes)

clown, a contrary figure of humour and sanctity— were powerful healers and great entertainers.

On the fourth night the ceremonies continued until dawn, when the puberty rite shaman painted on his palm a sun symbol which he pressed to the girl's head as the sun rose. She then performed another four ritual circles, the ceremonial tipi being dismantled as she ran. The hiring of the various skilled ceremonialists (who might be masters of up to 80 complex chants), the feeding of the spectators, and the dressing of the maiden represented an expensive undertaking for the girl's family; but the puberty rite was considered a vital, sacred confirmation of the beginning of womanhood.

The Jicarilla termed their traditional rituals 'long life' ceremonies, which, aside from the puberty rite, included the curative Holiness Rite and the Ceremonial Relay. The Holiness Rite, which featured the most arduous shamanic rôle, the impersonation of the Bear and Snake, the obscene performance of black- and brown-striped clowns, and the depositing of sickness on a ritually prepared tree, was performed to cure the powerful Snake and Bear sicknesses.

The Relay Race was representative of the dual food supply, and featured the sacred sand paintings used also by the Western Apache and Navajo. Ritually painted runners from the Ollero band, representing Sun and the animals, raced the Llanero athletes, who symbolised Moon and the

Qua-tha-hooly-hooly or Quatha-hooa-hooba (Yellow Face), a scout, photographed in a studio, probably in 1886. While his costume could easily be that of an Apache scout, he is in fact identified as a Mojave, sometimes called Apache-Mojave, and thus belongs to the Yuman linguistic group of the South-West. He wears a cartridge belt and holds a US Army revolver. Note the large awl-case, decorated with tin cone pendants and beadwork, hanging from the left side of his belt: such cases were popular among the Apaches. (Arizona State Museum, University of Arizona) plants. If the Olleros won, game would be abundant that year, while a Llanero victory symbolised success in gathering plants. Such ceremonies, stemming from myths and integrated into Apache culture, were profuse before the intervention of the white man.

The Apache Wars

The Spaniards

Drawn by the prospect of converts to the Roman Catholic faith and by the legends of mineral riches, the Spanish conquistadores inevitably ventured beyond their northern frontier in Mexico into the lands of the Apaches. When Francisco Vasquez de Coronado's expedition plundered the pueblos of the Rio Grande in 1540 the Apaches were well established in their traditional homeland in the South-West, although the eastern Apaches were divided into poorly defined bands on the borders of the Plains. Various subsequent expeditions continued to advertise the brutality of Spanish colonialism, and set the pattern of Spanish soldiers raiding to acquire Indian slaves, under the guise of extending the boundaries of civilisation. The capture of Indians for sale in the thriving slave market obviously did nothing to enrich relations between Apache and Spaniard.

In 1598 Juan de Onate, the first Spanish governor of New Mexico, founded a colony in the Rio Grande valley. In 1599 his soldiers attacked the Acoma Pueblo of the Keres, killing 800 and capturing nearly 600; whereupon he barbarously sentenced captured males over the age of 25 to have one foot cut off and to serve 20 years of slavery. It seems likely that Apaches, allies of the Keres, were present in the defence of Acoma. Certainly, in the years that followed, Apache or Navajo raided Onate's first capital at San Gabriel with such ferocity that it was moved to Santa Fé in 1610. By 1630 the Apaches were using horses both for mount and food, and a familiar pattern of conflict with the Spaniards had developed. When Apaches came to trade with the Pueblo Indians, the Spanish trapped them and sold them into slavery. The Apaches consequently nurtured a burning hatred for the Spanish and Mexicans, and retaliated with raids destructive and frequent enough to cause the abandonment of many settlements. While the sedentary Pueblos faced confiscation of crops or annihilation by superior arms if they challenged Spanish supremacy, the elusively mobile Apaches could strike viciously and recoil swiftly, using their ancient skills to evade pursuit.

To a degree, the Spanish invasion altered the Apaches' subsistence practices. Larger raiding parties were required, and families could no longer be left undefended; so, raiding became a constant practice for the whole local group, and stolen livestock compensated, to a certain extent, for the disrupted gathering of plants. Raiders frequently refrained from destroying settlements outright: while they remained they were a valuable economic resource—the Spaniards produced livestock and grain, which the Apache raiders duly collected.

Apache ambushes and raids were frequent from 1660 to 1680, when the Pueblo Revolt, abetted by some Apache groups, drove the Spanish from New Mexico. Despite the Spanish reconquest 12 years

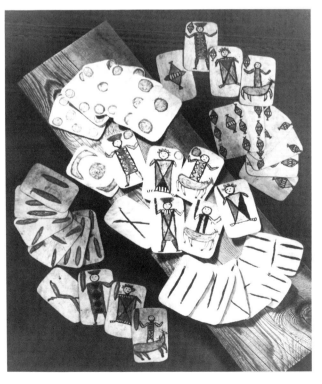

Apache rawhide playing cards, derived from Spanish models, showing the typical deck of four ten-card suits: clockwise from bottom left, the suits are clubs, coins, cups and swords. Each suit runs from ace to seven, with picture cards representing a page, mounted knight and king, in designs of red, yellow and black paint. (Arizona State Museum, University of Arizona: photo Helga Teiwes)

later, and the establishment of presidios along the northern frontier, the Apaches continued to raid deep into Mexico and Texas. By 1700 each tribe was firmly established in its traditional territory, and the pattern of raids and Spanish punitive expeditions continued throughout the 18th century. The Spanish used auxiliaries from tribes such as the Opata to bolster their defences. After 1714 Jicarilla Apaches were also used as auxiliaries, and were part of the force which defeated the Comanche in 1779.

After 1786 the Spanish departed from their impotent policy of extermination against the Apaches, when Viceroy Bernardo de Gálvez introduced a new approach. Tribes were to be encouraged to wage war against one another; and those seeking peace were to be settled on reservations—'establecimiento de paz'—near the Spanish presidios, and supplied with rations and inferior Spanish firearms to make them dependent upon the Spaniards. Gálvez also recommended supplying the Apaches with alcohol, as '. . . a means of gaining their goodwill, discovering their secrets,

Western Apache 'Pinal-Coyotero' delegation, San Carlos Reservation, Arizona, before 1877: *left to right:* Napasgingush, wife of Eskinilay, Cullah, Eskinilay, Passalah, Pinal and son, Hautsuhnehay, Eskayelah, Skellegunney, and Cushshashado. (Arizona State Museum, University of Arizona)

calming them so they will think less often of conceiving and executing their hostilities, and creating for them a new necessity which will oblige them to recognise their dependence upon us more directly'.

The new policy enjoyed moderate success, leading to a period of relative calm from 1790 to 1830. Chiricahua groups settled near Bacoachi in 1786 (although their most friendly chief, Isosé, was killed by hostile Chiricahuas in 1788). Peaceful Indians joined the Spaniards in pursuing the hostiles, illustrating Spanish success in breaking tribal strength. Similarly, the alliance between Apache and Navajo was ruptured after Gileños killed the Navajo chief Antonio El Pinto for helping the Spanish against them. By 1793 eight reservations contained as many as 2,000 Apaches, and in 1810 the Mescalero were granted land rights and rations.

The Mexicans

After the declaration of Mexican Independence the Apache situation deteriorated. The Mexican government could not afford to man the presidios efficiently, and their lack of funds reduced subsidies for the system of supplying rations to the Apaches, undermining any treaties between the Apaches and the Mexicans. Raiding was resumed with great ferocity in the 1830s, depopulating much of poorly defended northern Sonora and Chihuahua.

The deeply-ingrained Apache hatred of the Mexicans was intensified when, in 1825, the

governor of Sonora offered a bounty of 100 pesos ($100) for the scalp of any Apache warrior over fourteen. This bounty was imitated by Chihuahua province in 1837, and was even extended to 50 pesos for women's scalps and 25 pesos for those of children.

In 1822 the Mexicans had resumed working the copper mines at Santa Rita, under the protection of Juan José Compá, leader of the Coppermine Mimbreños. In 1837 Juan José was invited by an American trader called James Johnson, whom he believed to be a trusted friend, to attend a feast. The chief complied; but as his people ate and drank, Johnson fired a hail of grapeshot from a concealed howitzer into their midst, and his armed associates then completed the bloody massacre. Juan José's

A 1981 Apache Puberty Rite on the San Carlos Reservation Watched by her sponsor, and accompanied by the beating drums, the maiden seeks the blessing of the sun; a piece of abalone shell in her hair symbolising her rôle as White Shell Woman. (Arizona State Museum, University of Arizona)

Apache scouts at Fort Wingate, New Mexico, on parade with 45/70 carbines and web-type cartridge belts. (US Signal Corps)

scalp was among the many that Johnson and his fellow bounty hunters subsequently carried to Sonora to exchange for their blood money.

Juan José's successor was Mangas Coloradas—Red Sleeves—a huge man with a mane of black hair, renowned as a warrior and statesman. He vented his fury against the Mexican settlers at Santa Rita by waylaying the 'conducta' which supplied them with provisions. As the settlers were forced to abandon the safety of the fort they were killed by the Mimbreño warriors. The territory of the Mimbreños remained unsafe after the abandonment of Santa Rita, the scalp bounties naturally fuelling the bitter conflict between the Apaches and the Mexicans.

War with the Americans

After the signing of the Treaty of Guadalupe Hidalgo of 1848, ceding the Spanish South-West and its Indian tribes to the United States, American troops were withdrawn from Mexico. Despite the United States' agreement to stop the Apaches crossing the new border, the raids upon which the tribes had grown to depend continued. The Apaches failed to understand the Americans' attitude towards raiding into Mexico.

Cochise and Mangas Coloradas

In the aftermath of the 1851 Boundaries Commission, miners reopened the Santa Rita coppermines and discovered gold at nearby Pinos Altos. Mangas Coloradas reputedly visited the miners' camp and offered to lead them to greater gold deposits. Fearing a trap, they bound the great chief to a tree and whipped him brutally. His rage made him an implacable enemy of the Americans in the years to come. After the 1853 Gadsen Purchase Apache distrust grew and spread, as an increasing number of American settlers entered their lands. The attention of the Americans was focused on the Chiricahuas who, although friendly enough to safeguard the passage of the Butterfield Stage, provided the main obstacle to American settlement of New Mexico.

In January 1861 Lt. George Bascom of the 7th Infantry led 54 mounted infantrymen to Apache Pass, seeking the return of two kidnapped boys. Cochise, the great leader of the Central Chiricahua, was asked to come to Bascom's tent, and arrived at the head of a small group. He suggested that the boys had been kidnapped by Coyotero Apaches, and offered to intervene. Bascom wrongly accused Cochise of the crime, however, insisting that he

135

would be held prisoner until the boys were returned. Alarmed and angry, the chief instantly drew a knife, slashed the tent, and escaped the soldiers who had gathered around him; but the other Chiricahuas were held as hostages. Cochise returned with his own hostages—captured Butterfield Mail employees—and offered to exchange them for his own people. In an atmosphere of mutual distrust, Cochise's followers and Bascom's troops became involved in a brief skirmish, and both men killed their hostages.

In the years that followed, the US troops were withdrawn from the Apache's lands to fight the Civil War. Cochise took this opportunity, assisted by Mangas Coloradas, to drive the settlers away by relentless raiding. Treaties were abandoned, and once again an extermination policy was adopted against the Apaches. In 1862 Gen. James Carleton's California Volunteers repossessed New Mexico and Arizona from the Confederates. A despatch unit under Capt. Roberts was sent through Apache Pass, where Cochise and Mangas Coloradas lay in wait.

The artillery accompanying the soldiers defeated the ambush, however, and Mangas Coloradas was shot from his horse. He was carried to Janos, where doctors were told to cure him or their town would be destroyed. He survived; but a year later ventured, under a flag of truce, into the camp of Capt. Shirland's California Volunteers, to parley for peace with the miners and soldiers. He was seized as a prisoner, and Gen. West reputedly told his guards: 'I want him dead or alive tomorrow morning do you understand? I want him dead'. The guards were seen during the night heating their bayonets and placing them on the ageing chief's legs; when he remonstrated, they shot him. To complete their work they decapitated him, and boiled his head in a large, black pot. The official report explained that Mangas Coloradas was killed 'while attempting to escape'. Cochise fought on, with such warriors as Nana and Victorio of the Warm Springs Apaches by his side.

Carleton's campaigns, in which 'the Indians are to be soundly whipped', were also aimed at the Mescalero and Navajo; and his inflexible policy resulted in the massacre of Manuelito's peaceful Mescalero band in 1862. The two tribes were rounded up and concentrated at the Bosque

Scouts, possibly Yuman, with US Army officers. The uniformed scout, Na-da-sa, wears a Mills cartridge-belt and holds a Springfield rifle. (Arizona State Museum, University of Arizona)

136

Apache Gan Dancers:
1: Western Apache
2: Mescalero Apache
3: Chiricahua Apache

A

Chiricahua Apache:
1, 2, 4, 6: Warriors
3, 5: Women

B

Chiricahua Puberty Ceremony:
1: Maiden
2: Sponsor
3: Shaman

C

Western Apache:
1,2: San Carlos warriors
3: Tonto warrior
4: Western Apache fiddle player

5, 8: Western Apache women
6: Western Apache shaman
7: White Mountain woman

D

Mescalero Apache:
1, 2: Warriors
3: Woman

E

Jicarilla Apache:
1, 2: Warriors
3: Woman

F

Apache Scouts:
1, 2, 4: Scouts
3: 1st Sgt. of Scouts

G

Redondo Reservation, despite its unsuitability and their mutual hostility. By 1865 some 9,000 Navajo and 500 Mescaleros were concentrated there in appalling conditions; and the Mescaleros began to slip back to their old lands as Carleton sought unsuccessfully to imprison even more tribes on the reservation. In 1868 the Navajos were permitted to make the joyous 'Long Walk' back to their own country.

Crook's First Campaign

In 1870 President Grant's 'peace policy' provided an alternative to extermination, and was given added impetus by the 1871 Camp Grant Massacre. Peaceful Arivaipa Apache women and children under Eskiminzin were massacred by Tucson citizens and Papago Indians, and the outrages committed created a national outcry. Gen. George Crook was appointed commander of the Depart-ment of Arizona, to put an end to the fumblings of military and civilian authorities and to enforce settlement of the Apaches on reservations. A peace commission under Vincent Colyer and Gen. Oliver Howard was meanwhile sent to establish the reservations.

Reservations were established at Fort Apache for the Cibecue and northern White Mountain; at Camp Verde for the northern and southern Tonto; and at Camp Grant for the San Carlos and southern White Mountain divisions of the Western Apache tribe. Outbreaks and raids continued, however; and in 1872 Crook embarked on his Tonto Basin campaign. He used the tactics which were to prove so successful in subduing the Apaches, most

Western Apache 'Coyotero' warriors, including the chief Al-che-say, armed with Springfield and Winchester carbines. Note the feathered buckskin war-caps. (**Arizona State Museum, University of Arizona**)

An impressive photograph of US and Apache scouts, under Lt. Maus, 1886, showing variations in scout costumes. (**Arizona State Museum, University of Arizona**)

particularly by using Apache scouts to harass the hostiles tirelessly, and to demonstrate that they had no place to hide. It became a popular saying that only an Apache could catch an Apache, and Crook once commented: 'To polish a diamond, there is nothing like its own dust'. Part of the reason for Crook's success with his scouts, and in all his dealings with the Apaches, was that they trusted him. He told them the truth, and honesty was a very important virtue among the Apaches.

The most dramatic battle fought against the Tontos was that at Salt River Cave in December 1872. Maj. Brown's column trapped the Apaches in a huge, shallow cave 400 to 500 feet from the top of a cliff. It was seemingly unassailable, being protected by a natural rampart; and the Tontos slapped their buttocks and jeered derisively when asked to surrender. By firing at the cave roof, however, the soldiers ricocheted their bullets down on to the Tonto families. Suddenly, a high-pitched, despairing, yet threatening wail filled the air, which the scouts identified as the death song, meaning that the Apaches were about to charge. The charge was repelled by the soldiers' rapid-fire musketry, and the Apaches were beaten. A similar victory on Turret Mountain secured the surrender of the majority of the Tontos. Crook put a price on the head of the most irreconcilable warrior, Delshay,

An 1885 studio shot of White Mountain Apache Scouts: *left to right:* **Das-Luca, Skro-Kit, and Shus-El-Day. They are a magnificent example of the variety seen among Apache scouts' uniforms. All carry Springfield carbines. (Arizona State Museum, University of Arizona)**

and two scouts submitted separate heads. 'Being satisfied that both parties were earnest in their beliefs, and the bringing in of an extra head as not amiss, I paid both parties', Crook explained.

By 1870 many Eastern Chiricahuas, including Loco and Victorio, had gathered at Cañada Alamosa Agency near Ojo Caliente (Warm Springs), weary of war. When ordered to move to the Tualarosa Reservation, however, they fled into the mountains. In 1872 Gen. Howard and Thomas Jeffords (a friend of Cochise's since he ventured alone into the Chiricahua stronghold) established a reservation for Cochise's people around the Chiricahua Mountains. It was troubled by visits from Chiricahuas and White Mountain Apaches unhappily situated at Tualarosa and San Carlos, and by its close proximity to the border. Cochise's death in 1874 coincided with requests for the Chiricahua to move to Warm Springs, following the failure of the Cañada Alamosa Agency.

The work of settling the Indians peacefully on reservations was largely undone by the 'concentration' policy implemented after 1875. By virtue of the Indians' love for their own lands, and the enmity between many tribes, a concentration policy inevitably provoked trouble. In February 1875 over 1,400 Tontos and Yavapais made a terrible mountain journey to San Carlos; Levi Edwin Dudley, who supervised the removal, snapped: 'They are Indians—let the beggars walk'. They were joined there by the White Mountain band from Fort Apache in July.

Clum and Victorio

The San Carlos Reservation was run by John P. Clum, whose independent actions, aided by his Apache police, created great conflict with the military. In 1876 Clum arrived to escort the 1,000 Chiricahuas from the Chiricahua Reservation to San Carlos, though many—including the most prominent hostiles Geronimo, Juh (Whoa) and Nolgee—had fled. They took refuge at the Warm Springs Reservation; but in 1877 Clum and his Indian police arrived there and, despite the late arrival of their military back-up, captured Geronimo and escorted the Chiricahuas to San Carlos.

Feeling that his authority was being usurped by the military, Clum resigned in July 1877; and in

Studio shot of an Apache Scout, labelled 'Apache Scout Mike'. He wears distinctive jewellery and face-paint, and holds a Springfield rifle. (Arizona State Museum, University of Arizona)

September, 300 Chiricahuas fled behind Victorio and Loco. Eleven days later 187 of them, including Victorio, surrendered at Fort Wingate, and were taken to Warm Springs, where more hostiles gradually convened. In mid-October 1878, they learned that they were to be escorted back to San Carlos, and Victorio and 80 followers scattered into the hills. In February 1879 Victorio surrendered at Mescalero; but in July, fearing arrest, he fled once again, this time to Mexico. A series of bloody raids followed, and Victorio evaded all attempts at pursuit. Eventually, on 15 October 1880, he died along with most of his warriors in a long battle with Mexican troops. Ironically, just before his flight it had been virtually decided to give the Chiricahua the Warm Springs Reservation which Victorio desired; but his raids caused the suspension of the idea. Victorio's war was continued by the ageing war leader and shaman Nana, whose 40 raiders won eight pitched battles and eluded 1,400 troops during two months of raiding in the summer of 1881, covering 1,000 miles before escaping into Mexico.

In 1881 many despairing San Carlos Indians had turned to the religion of a White Mountain shaman called Nocadelklinny, whose beliefs were reminiscent of the Plains Indian Ghost Dance. Against a backdrop of reservation boredom in the sterile, humid, disease-ridden atmosphere of San Carlos, he exercised enough influence to bring together Indians from hostile tribal groups. Fearing his anti-white preaching, the Americans ordered Nocadelklinny's arrest. On 30 August 1881 Col. Carr's troops, having secured the shaman's arrest, were attacked by a crowd of his followers, and the White Mountain scouts mutinied. On 1 September Apaches besieged Fort Apache; but the clamour died down, and the Indians disappeared overnight.

Crook and Geronimo

The dramatic increase in the military presence at San Carlos provoked the outbreak of Chiricahuas including Juh, Chato Naiche and Geronimo. Geronimo, a shaman and warrior of the Bedonkohe band, had been hardened for war from an early age by the Mexican massacre of his family; he consequently had a particular loathing for Mexicans, whom he used to boast that he killed 'with rocks'. Through his association with Juh and his

Nednhi Apaches, who formed part of the hostile band that roamed the Sierra Madre, Geronimo had earned a fearsome reputation by 1880.

In April 1882 Juh and Geronimo secretly slipped back onto the reservation and forcefully persuaded Loco's people to flee with them. The chief of Indian police, Albert Sterling, was shot dead, and Geronimo led the group of several hundred Chiricahuas away from the agency. Pursued by troops including cavalry under Col. George Forsyth, the Apaches—supposedly protected by Geronimo's power to delay the coming of daylight—reached the Mexican border. Relaxing their vigilance, however, they stumbled into a Mexican ambush, and suffered severe casualties. Even Apaches were not infallible.

In September 1882 Gen. Crook resumed command of the Department of Arizona, and listened to the grievances of the San Carlos Apaches. He stationed a cavalry unit at San Carlos to prevent the hostiles sneaking back, and organised his mule trains and five companies of White Mountain Apache scouts to pursue the raiders. His force of 50 soldiers was dwarfed by the presence of 200 Apache scouts, who wore scarlet headbands to

A posed photograph of a US scouting party in the field. Note the gauntlets, sacred feather war-medicine caps, and the crouching position of the front Apache scout. They are armed with Springfield rifles. (Arizona State Museum, University of Arizona)

identify themselves as they crossed the border into Mexico—which was now permitted under a new 'hot pursuit' agreement between the Mexicans and Americans.

In March 1883 the hostiles unleashed lightning raids into Mexico, south-east Arizona and New Mexico. On 1 May 1883 Crook's Sierra Madre Expedition commenced; and, guided by a scout known as Peaches who had lived with the hostiles, the force followed the raiders as they recoiled into their Sierra Madre fortress. The scouts, under Capt. Emmett Crawford, scaled the rugged range in advance of the main party, guided by refuse from old camps, and by signs of dances. They surrounded the hostiles' main mountain camp as best they could and captured it, killing nine people, while most of the renegade men were away raiding.

Impressed by Crook, and feeling that they could trust him, the renegade Apaches surrendered after Geronimo had made three long parleys. Crook then escorted over 325 Apaches back to San Carlos, but

Geronimo and his band of hostiles shortly before their surrender to Crook, 1886: excellent reference of Apache costume actually worn in the field. Note the variety of weapons and headbands, typical face-paint, and unusual war-cap; and the costume and spy-glass case of Cochise's son Naiché on the far right. (Arizona State Museum, University of Arizona)

accepted Geronimo's word that he would come in himself when he had gathered all his people. To many people's surprise, Geronimo repaid Crook's trust, arriving in March 1884 (driving a huge herd of stolen Mexican cattle, which were duly confiscated). Such hardened renegades as Chihuahua, Nana, Loco, Chato and Geronimo were now on the reservation; while the irreconcilable Juh had drowned during the autumn of 1883.

In May 1885, however, following a bout of illegal tiswin-drinking, Geronimo, fearing his rumoured arrest, bolted from San Carlos accompanied by Chihuahua; Naiche, son of Cochise; Nana; and Mangas, son of Mangas Coloradas. A telegram warning Crook of the escape was filed, and failed to reach him. Chihuahua split from the other Apaches, and was pursued by Lt. Davis into Mexico. Crook meanwhile placed cavalry along the border at all water holes, and organised a pursuit by Apache scouts as Geronimo again sought the refuge of the Sierra Madre. In January Crawford's scouts captured the hostiles' horses and provisions, and opened negotiations with Geronimo; but Crawford was then shot and killed by Mexican scalp-hunters, a murder for which his scouts sought furious vengeance.

Threatened by American and Mexican soldiers, and relentlessly harassed by the scouts, on 25 March 1886 Geronimo parleyed with Crook, and with

Chato and Alchise who had accompanied the general. On condition that they would be allowed to return to their families after two years' imprisonment in the East, Geronimo said: 'Once I moved about like the wind. Now I surrender to you—and that is all'. The War Department reneged on Crook's terms, however, their demand for unconditional surrender placing Crook in an impossible position. Thirty-nine hostile Chiricahuas under Geronimo and Naiche had meanwhile fled once more after being supplied with whiskey by a trader. At the suggestion that his Apache scouts had colluded in the affair, Crook resigned in disgust on 1 April and was replaced by Brig.-Gen. Nelson ('Bear Coat') Miles. The 77 fugitive Chiricahuas who had surrendered were entrained for Fort Marion, Oklahoma and arrived on 13 April 1886.

Miles unleashed hundreds of scouts and 5,000 soldiers—about one-third of the army's strength on the frontier—after 20 warriors and 13 women. Ultimately, two scouts secured a parley; and on 4 September 1886 Geronimo surrendered for the last time. In the course of 1885–86 his band had inflicted some 95 casualties on the US Army and American civilians, and killed an unknown number of Mexicans; Geronimo's losses are thought to have totalled 13, few if any to direct US Army action. He and his warriors were sent to Fort Pickens, Florida in 1886, while their families went to Fort Marion. Under Miles, even the peaceful Chiricahuas were dispatched to the overcrowded Florida forts, 381 being sent in September 1886. Among those held there were Crook's loyal scouts, who had been promised a payment of ten ponies rather than incarceration.

In 1887 a loyal scout known as the Apache Kid was imprisoned for shooting the killer of his father, but escaped and eluded capture until his reported death in the Sierra Madre from tuberculosis in 1894. The luckless Arivaipa Eskiminzin, was accused of aiding the Apache Kid and, without Crook's protection, was also exiled from his prospering fields to Florida.

The Chiricahua were moved to Mt. Vernon Barracks, Alabama, in 1887 and 1888, though this was little improvement. In 1894 they were moved to Fort Sill, Oklahoma, where Geronimo died on 17 February 1909. The Western Apache groups remained at San Carlos Reservation, while the Jicarilla were granted a reservation in Rio Arriba in 1880. The Mescalero finally received title to their lands on the eastern slopes of the White and Sacramento Mountains in 1922. The Lipan had moved to the Mescalero Reservation in 1903. In 1913 the Chiricahuas in Oklahoma were finally given their freedom: 84 of them continued to farm their lands at Fort Sill, while 187 returned at last to the South-West's Apacheria, and lived on the Mescalero Reservation.

The Plates

A: Apache Gan Dancers

The costume of the *gan* dancers invoked the supernatural power of the Mountain Spirits, principally for curative ceremonies and to ward off evil; and was based upon the presiding shaman's vision of the *gan*, and each dancer's personal designs.

A1: Western Apache gan dancer

A bandana holds in place his black-dyed cloth hood, which has holes cut for eyes and mouth, plus false 'eyes' of silver buttons. Breathing was clearly very difficult, and the *gan* dancers required frequent rests. Above the mask, and painted with sacred designs, is the yucca rack, called 'horns' by the Apache in reference to the *gans'* rôle as protectors of game. Like the painted, slatted yucca wands held in the hands, it is very elaborate, as was typical among the Western Apache. His body-paint, and arm-trailers of rawhide and red cloth with eagle feathers, are further symbols of power. He wears traditional *gan* costume of fringed buckskin kilt with tin cone janglers and brass bells, beaded knee-high moccasins with disc toes, and a wide leather belt decorated with silver conches, brass tacks and bells.

A2: Mescalero Apache gan dancer

He wears a dyed cloth mask with silver button 'eyes', a bandana, and a painted rack topped with a dyed eagle 'fluffy'. The tin disc at the centre of the rack symbolises Sun; the wooden drops at the ends of the horns, Rain; and the paint designs on rack, wands, mask and body are symbolic of such supernaturals as Stars, Lightning and the Four Directions. Streamers of cloth and eagle feathers

A 1900s photograph of an old Apache woman fiercely fleshing a buckskin, included more for evocative atmosphere than costume detail. (Arizona State Museum, University of Arizona)

swirl from his arms. He wears knee-high buckskin, disc-toe moccasins, a buckskin kilt decorated with tin cones and beadwork, and a tacked leather belt.

A3: Chiricahua Apache gan dancer

His traditional mask of buckskin—dyed, painted, and held in place with a cloth bandana—has a cluster of rattlesnake rattles (here hidden at the back). The typical painted, slatted rack, topped with dyed eagle 'fluffies', has wooden pendants symbolising rain, and turkey feathers at its base invoking the Mountain Spirits. His arms are adorned with red flannel trailers and brass bells, and his body with sacred paint designs. He carries typically simple Chiricahua wands; and wears a leather belt with silver conches, and knee-high buckskin disc-toe moccasins. His fringed buckskin kilt is decorated with tin pendants, and cut to create ornate fringes below the belt.

A young Apache woman wearing a traditional costume of necklaces and painted buckskin blouse, with fringing, beadwork and tin cone pendants, worn over a cotton skirt. Apache baskets and a pitch-covered water jar comprise the studio props. (Arizona State Museum, University of Arizona)

B1: Chiricahua warrior

An archetypal Apache warrior: he wears a cloth headband, white-stripe war paint, bead necklace, neckerchief tied with a silver conch, cotton shirt, loose cotton drawers, breechclout, and boot-length buckskin moccasins bound above the calf. Over a buttoned waistcoat of corduroy he wears a war medicine thong of shell and beads slung from his right shoulder and holding a beaded 'ration-ticket pouch' fringed with tin cones. Tweezers (for plucking facial hair) hang from a thong around his neck. He carries an 1873 Winchester carbine, decorated with brass tacks. He has two cartridge-belts; one, decorated with red paint, supports a holster which holds a 'pearl'-handled Colt double-action 'Frontier' Model 1878, a thong hanging from the lanyard-ring on the butt. A buckskin serves as the horse's saddle, and the bridle is leather decorated with brass tacks and silver.

B2: Chiricahua warrior

He wears a cotton shirt, loose cotton drawers, breechclout, moccasins, cartridge belt, and a headband in distinctive folded style. His beaded necklace centres on a silver conch, and a mirror forms a part of his sacred, beaded war-medicine thong. He is armed with a .45/70 Springfield rifle.

B3: Chiricahua woman

She wears a cotton blouse and skirt, leather conch-belt, beaded bracelets, and a necklace of beads and shells with conch pendant. Her face is daubed with paint; and she holds a sling—a traditional Apache weapon.

B4: Chiricahua warrior

His distinctive war-cap, with paint designs and rawhide 'ears', invokes supernatural protection in battle. He wears a heavy jacket over a cotton shirt, breechclout and moccasins, and his neckerchief threads through silver conches and is hung with beads. Armed with a .45/70 Springfield carbine, he wears a conch-belt and a cartridge-belt.

B5: Chiricahua woman

Wearing a cotton blouse and typical bead

necklaces, she has daubed across her face the white stripe considered so typical of the Chiricahua men.

B6: Chiricahua warrior

In contrast to much Mexican-influenced costume, he wears more traditional garb of headband, conch and bead necklace, moccasins, and breechclout hung over a belt—this being typically narrow at the front, long and wrapped wide at the back. He carries a lance, deerskin quiver and bow case decorated with red flannel, and a 'flop-head' club: a club encased in rawhide with a slashed section between the stone head and wooden handle, to make it flexible and to prevent the club from breaking upon impact.

C: Chiricahua Puberty Ceremony

With the sacred tipi in the background, the maiden's sponsor pushes her away to make four ritual runs, accompanied by the presiding shaman's singing. Cattail fronds—symbols of renewal—carpet the ground.

C1: Puberty rite maiden

She is dressed to represent White Painted Woman, who is invoked by the abalone shell in her beaded necklaces. The girl's ritually-prepared deerskin dress is decorated with fringing, brass buttons, tin cone pendants, and beadwork designs representing her protective supernaturals. Like the beaded deerskin disc-toe moccasins, the dress is coloured yellow to symbolise pollen, which is also smeared over the maiden's face. She wears a scratcher and drinking tube on a thong around her neck.

C2: Chiricahua puberty rite sponsor

An older woman of unquestionable reputation, she wears typical Chiricahua costume: a patterned cotton blouse, skirt, wide leather belt, moccasins, and necklaces of seeds.

C3: Chiricahua puberty rite shaman

He wears a cotton shirt, a two-string medicine thong strung with shells, beads, turquoise and *hoddentin* pouch, and a buckskin medicine hat decorated with the horns and fur of a prong-horned deer, felt symbols and tassels, paint designs and a horsehair fringe at the back (based upon an example in the Museum of the American Indian,

New York). His left hand is painted with a Sun symbol, and his right hand clutches a deer dew-claw rattle.

D: Western Apache

Wagering on games was a favourite pastime of the Apaches, and the use of rawhide playing cards adapted from Spanish decks became a distinctive Apache trait. Both men and women played such card games as 'monte'; in contrast, the men's popular 'hoop and pole' game was sacred and could not be witnessed by women.

D1: San Carlos warrior

He wears a cloth headband, under which passes a thin buckskin band war-amulet, braided into the hair and decorated with shell. His fringed buckskin war shirt is decorated with beadwork, brass tacks, and crosses and raised discs or conches of German silver. Spanish/Mexican influence is shown in the

An 1880s studio shot showing White Mountain Apache women's costume, and the man's feathered war-cap and use of blanket. (Arizona State Museum, University of Arizona)

loose white cotton drawers and striped socks, as seen in many contemporary photographs. He also wears typical Western Apache moccasins, with upturned discs on the toes; and a cloth breechclout. The Apaches were compulsive gamblers, and would even wager their metal identification tags (which Crook had introduced to distinguish between reservation and 'hostile' Indians).

D2: San Carlos warrior

He wears a patterned headband and a buckskin band war-amulet decorated with beadwork, metal plates and shells, again braided into the hair. The elaborate war-shirt, decorated with fringing, brass tacks and intricate beadwork, is worn over a

patterned shirt. His jewellery consists of a bead necklace with three drops of silver discs and a silver cross; a cluster of bracelets made from beads and cowrie shells; and a collection of silver rings. He also wears cotton drawers, breechclout, disc-toe moccasins decorated with beadwork; and a reservation identification tag hanging by a chain from his necklace.

D3: Tonto warrior

He wears a breeechclout, moccasins, beaded bracelets, and a sacred medicine cord. This latter comprises four intertwined thongs of dyed buckskin strung with beads, shells, pieces of turquoise, and rattlesnake rattles, and holds a buckskin bag of *hoddentin*. Such cords might consist of one, two, three or four thongs, and were important as shamans' paraphernalia and warriors' protective amulets.

US Army officer and band of unidentified Apache scouts armed with Springfield rifles. (Arizona State Museum, University of Arizona)

His war-cap of clipped turkey and two eagle feathers imparted protection and swiftness in battle, and is based upon an example in the Musem of the American Indian, New York.

D4: Western Apache fiddle player

He wears a breechclout, cotton drawers, shirt, waistcoat, headband, neckerchief, necklace of beads and cowrie shells, and wide leather belt with silver conches. His Apache fiddle, crafted from the painted stalk of a mescal plant and played socially rather than ceremonially, was most typically found among the Western Apache. The fiddle, like the wooden bow, is strung with horsehair, and is small in comparison to those examples later made purely for trade.

D5: Western Apache woman

Wearing typical full blouse and skirt, and necklaces of trade beads and mirrors, she uses a headstrap to carry a twined burden basket. Decorated with paint designs, leather fringes and tin cone pendants, and strengthened by a rawhide base, the basket could also be hung from a horse's saddle.

Geronimo and Naiché, mounted; Geronimo's son holding a baby by his side; and a fourth unidentified Apache, shortly before their surrender to Crook in 1886. (Robin May Collection)

D6: Western Apache shaman

The shaman wears the paraphernalia invoking his power to perform curative ceremonies. His medicine shirt, a folded buckskin rectangle with a head-hole, is painted with symbols representing his power, hung with shells, and worn over a cotton shirt. His wands, representing the Four Directions, are hung with eagle feathers and painted with designs including the Snake; this supernatural is also the central feature of his medicine hat (based upon an example in the Museum of the American Indian, New York). Other ceremonial objects are carried in his painted, fringed buckskin medicine bag.

D7: White Mountain Apache woman

She wears beaded earrings, skirt, and patterned blouse. Contemporary photographs show that both men and women wore cartridge belts, and hanging from hers is a sheath holding a butcher knife. Her hair is folded up into a leather '*nah-leen*' or hair-bow decorated with beadwork, brass tacks and long, bright ribbons, indicating that she is eligible for marriage.

D8: Western Apache woman
Wearing cotton blouse and skirt, and a necklace of beads with a mirror pendant, she demonstrates the method of carrying the cradleboard, which has protective amulets hung around the hood.

E: Mescalero Apache:
E1: Mounted Mescalero warrior
He wears a waistcoat, cotton shirt, fringed leggings decorated with brass studs, beaded moccasins of the Plains type, and a blanket around his waist. The buckskin war-cap—decorated with a checked beadwork browband, beadwork top, a bead-wrapped horsehair pendant and dyed feathers—has an unusual Plains-like trailer of eagle feathers on a buckskin strip decorated with painted bird and animal symbols (after an example in the Museum of the American Indian, New York). He wears typically long silver earrings; and carries a painted medicine shield, and a fringed quiver and bowcase, decorated with cloth and beadwork, made from the prized skin of a mountain lion. The horse wears a captured US Army bridle decorated with brass tacks.

E2: Mescalero warrior
He wears a fringed buckskin shirt decorated with painted symbols and tin cone pendants; cloth wrapped around his waist; fringed moccasins embellished with beadwork and tin cone pendants;

Geronimo and his band *en route* **to a Florida prison camp, 1886. (Robin May Collection)**

and beaded, fringed buckskin leggings, based upon a pair in the Museum of the American Indian, New York. His open-topped fur turban, typical of the Mescalero, is decorated with cloth, pearl buttons, 'fluffies' and an eagle feather. A bear claw hangs from a thong around his neck; he carries a typically long-bladed lance decorated with cloth, beadwork and feathers, and a painted medicine shield.

E3: Mounted Mescalero woman with cradleboard

Both the cradleboard, hung with several protective amulets, and the woman's painted, beaded and fringed buckskin dress are based upon examples in the Museum of the American Indian, New York.

F: Jicarilla Apache:

F1: Jicarilla warrior

He wears Plains-type beaded moccasins, heavily fringed and beaded skin leggings, and a typically long trade-cloth breechclout. His buckskin shirt with long fringes and beaded panels, and his choker of leather studded with brass tacks and studs and hung with beads and shells, are based upon examples in the Museum of the American Indian, New York. He wears a Plains-type eagle feather upright-bonnet, with beaded browband; and beaded hair-tubes typical of the Jicarilla. He has smudged white war paint on to his cheeks, and carries a 'flop-head' club.

F2: Jicarilla warrior

A single eagle feather in his hair, this warrior too wears beaded hair-tubes, with distinctive face-paint, and hair-pipe bone choker and drop earrings. He holds an eagle feather fan. An otter skin is worn over the front of a fringed buckskin shirt, and a long breechclout with beaded cloth leggings and moccasins complete the costume.

F3: Jicarilla woman

Over a cloth dress with added patterned hem she wears a typical, beautifully-beaded cape. Her leggings are beaded, but her moccasins, in common with most Jicarilla women's, are plain. Her hair is tied with yarn; and she wears face-paint, hair-pipe bone chokers, and necklaces of hair-pipe bone, beads and silver conches. She carries a basket, and wears the distinctive Jicarilla broad leather belt decorated with a brass chain and tacks.

Oliver Otis Howard, the one-armed, bible-toting 'praying general' who implemented Grant's 'peace policy' in the South-West. (Robin May Collection)

G: Apache Scouts

While US Army Apache scouts were issued with various uniforms, they usually wore a combination of Army clothing and traditional costume. The scouts here examine the dying embers of a camp fire, an abandoned 'wickiup' in the background.

G1: Apache Scout

He wears a US Army dress helmet, which was later—in 1890—issued to the scouts with the addition of a crossed arrows badge mounted on the staff plate. (It was issued as part of an official full dress uniform for the US Indian Scouts, whose branch-of-service colour became white piped with red.) The five-button fatigue jacket, trousers and boots are all Army issue. He has a tacked leather choker; leather gauntlets, first issued to mounted troops in about 1885; and an 1873 Winchester carbine.

G2: Apache Scout

His costume consists of Apache moccasins, breech-clout, bead and shell bracelets; and an issue Army blouse turned inside out for the sake of the grey lining's lower visibility. He wears a cartridge-belt supporting a butcher knife in a tacked sheath, and holds a Springfield carbine. His 'keyhole' identity tag's shape and number reveal his position in band and tribe and his rôle as a scout, in accordance with Crook's 1873 'tagging' policy. Supernatural power is invoked by the beaded medicine string, and the striking buckskin war-cap adorned with paint and owl feathers, based upon an example in the Museum of the American Indian, New York.

Three warriors, probably Tonto Apache, wearing traditional costume including distinctive war-caps, and carrying lance, bow and arrow, and Springfield rifle. (Robin May Collection)

G3: First Sergeant of Scouts
He bears the stripes of his rank (at this date, in cavalry yellow) on a five-button fatigue jacket, and wears the red headband which was considered regulation for scouts but which was actually far from universal. He is armed with a Springfield carbine.

G4: Apache Scout
He has cut the seat from his loose cotton drawers to create leggings, worn with moccasins, cotton breechclout, patterned shirt, waistcoat, and beaded bracelets. He is armed with an 1873 'trapdoor' Springfield .45/70 rifle, and wears the Mills

cartridge-belt. His buckskin war-cap is decorated with beadwork and eagle feathers, and based upon an example in the Museum of the American Indian.

G5: Apache Scout

He wears knee-high moccasins, cotton drawers, breechclout, typical striped trade shirt and cartridge-belt. The more incongruous influence from white culture is shown in the binocular case, white man's hat with upturned brim, and neatly knotted neck-tie.

Chato, possibly photographed in 1886—the Chiricahua leader who frequently fled the reservation to raid with Geronimo, but who in 1886 helped Crook to agree a parley with Geronimo's renegade band. Chato was one of the Chiricahuas who settled on the Mescalero Reservation in 1913. (Robin May Collection)

Bibliography

Adams, *Geronimo* (New English Library)

American Indian Art Magazine

Arizona Highways

Bahti, *Southwestern Indian Ceremonials* (KC)

Bahti, *Southwestern Indian Tribes* (KC)

Ball, *In The Days of Victorio* (Corgi)

Barrett, *Geronimo, His Own Story* (Abacus)

Bleeker, *The Apache Indians* (Dobson)

Bourke, *On The Border With Crook* (Time Life)

Brown, *Bury My Heart At Wounded Knee* (Pan)

Conn, *Robes of White Shell and Sunrise* (Denver Art Museum)

Cremony, *Life Among The Apaches* (Bison)

Davis, *The Truth About Geronimo* (Yale)

Debo, *Geronimo: The Man, His Time, His Place* (University of Oklahoma)

Forbes, *Apache, Navajo and Spaniard* (University of Oklahoma)

Handbook of North American Indians – 10 – Southwest (Smithsonian)

Hook, *The American Plains Indians* (Osprey)

Katcher, *The American Indian Wars 1860–1890* (Osprey)

Mails, *The People Called Apache* (Promontory)

May, *Indians* (Bison Books)

Mooney, *Calendar History of the Kiowa Indians* (Smithsonian)

Peterson and Elman, *The Great Guns* (Grosset and Dunlap)

Scherer, *Indians* (Bonanza)

Schmitt and Brown, *Fighting Indians of the West* (Charles Scribner's Sons)

Severn, *Conquering The Frontiers* (Foundation)

Sonnichsen, *The Mescalero Apaches* (University of Oklahoma)

Swanton, *The Indian Tribes of North America* (Smithsonian)

The Old West: The Great Chiefs (Time Life)

The Old West: The Indians (Time Life)

The Old West: The Scouts (Time Life)

The Old West: The Soldiers (Time Life)

The World of The American Indian (National Geographic)

Utley, *Bluecoats and Redskins* (Purnell)

Utley, *The History of The Indian Wars* (Mitchell Beazley)

Waldman and Braun, *The Atlas of The North American Indian* (Facts on File)

With Eagle Glance (Museum of The American Indian)

Worcester, *The Apaches, Eagles of the Southwest* (University of Oklahoma)

Articles

Chappell, *United States Scouts*.

Granfelt, *Apache Indian Identification Tags*.

Hoseney, *United States Scouts, 1890*.

Jacobsen, Jr, *The Uniform of the Indian Scouts*.

Lewis and Magruder, *Captain Crawford's Battalion of Apache Scouts, 1885*.

BESTSELLING MILITARY AND AVIATION SERIES FROM OSPREY

MEN-AT-ARMS
An unrivalled source of information on the uniforms and insignia of fighting units throughout history. Each 48-page book includes over 40 photographs and diagrams, and eight pages of full-color artwork.

NEW VANGUARD
Comprehensive histories of the design, development and operational use of the world's armoured vehicles and artillery. Each 48-page book contains eight pages of full-color artwork including a detailed cutaway.

WARRIOR
Definitive analysis of the appearance, weapons, equipment, tactics, character and conditions of service of the individual fighting man throughout history. Each 64-page book includes full-color uniform studies in close detail, and sectional artwork of the soldier's equipment.

ELITE
Detailed information on the organization, appearance and fighting record of the world's most famous military bodies. This series of 64-page books each contains some 50 photographs and diagrams and 10 full-color plates.

CAMPAIGN
Concise, authoritative accounts of history's decisive military encounters. Each 96-page book contains over 90 illustrations including maps, orders of battle, color plates, and three-dimensional battle maps.

ORDER OF BATTLE
The most detailed information ever published on the units which fought history's great battles. Each 96-page book contains comprehensive organization diagrams supported by ultra-detailed color maps. Each title also includes a large fold-out base map.

AIRCRAFT OF THE ACES
Focuses exclusively on the elite pilots of major air campaigns, and includes unique interviews with surviving aces. Each 96-page volume contains up to 40 specially commissioned color artworks, unit listings, new scale plans and the best archival photography available.

COMBAT AIRCRAFT
Technical information from the world's leading aviation writers on the century's most significant military aircraft. Each 96-page volume contains up to 40 specially commissioned color artworks, unit listings, new scale plans and the best archival photography available.